THE REALITY OF **ANGELIC MINISTRY** TODAY

BOOK ONE

DANCING WITH
ANGELS 1

THE REALITY OF **ANGELIC MINISTRY** TODAY

BOOK ONE

DANCING WITH
ANGELS 1

How to Work with the Angels in Your Life

KEVIN BASCONI

DESTINY IMAGE° PUBLISHERS, INC.

P.O. Box 310, Shippensburg, PA 17257-0310

"Speaking to the Purposes of God for This Generation and for the Generations to Come."

This book and all other Destiny Image, Revival Press, MercyPlace, Fresh Bread, Destiny Image Fiction, and Treasure House books are available at Christian bookstores and distributors worldwide.

For a U.S. bookstore nearest you, call 1-800-722-6774.

For more information on foreign distributors, call 717-532-3040.

Or reach us on the Internet: www.destinyimage.com.

Trade Paper ISBN 13: 978-0-7684-3689-1
Hardcover ISBN 13: 978-0-7684-3690-7
Large Print ISBN 13: 978-0-7684-3691-4
Ebook ISBN 13: 978-0-7684-9024-4

For Worldwide Distribution, Printed in the U.S.A.

1 2 3 4 5 6 7 8 9 10 11 / 14 13 12 11 10

Previous ISBN: 978-88-89127-90-2

Dedication

This book

is

dedicated

to

God the Father, God the Son, and God the Holy Spirit.

Without

You Guys,

of this

would

have

been

possible!

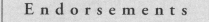

Endorsements

Kevin's insights are not just captivating; they are biblically faithful and true.

Angels not only played an important role in biblical history, but they continue to intervene in people's lives today. God's Word emphasizes great spiritual activity in the latter-days; Jesus Himself said, "The end-of-the-age is the harvest," and promised to send an angelic host to co-labor with us in the mandate to see Him receive the full measure of His reward. Kevin offers scriptural answers to many often-asked questions about angels.

This book can revolutionize your life, your family, and your ministry as you put into practice the teachings of Jesus as expounded and illustrated by Kevin and Kathy's incredible life and ministry.

Dancing With Angels 1 has my highest recommendation.

BRIAN LAKE
Brian Lake Ministries

There is a worldwide hunger for the supernatural realm and the ministry of angels today like never before.

In *Dancing With Angels 1*, Kevin Basconi takes the mystery out of angelic encounters and clearly shows that these super-natural experiences are for everyone, including you!

I know of few people who have the frequency and magnitude of angelic visitations as Kevin. He is well qualified to write this book. The amazing stories leave you hungry to have your own encounters with angels.

Angels have always been involved in our lives; we just have not been cognizant of them. Many people are now becoming more aware of their presence by seeing, feeling, and sensing the angels around them. You can too!

In Acts 12 Peter was freed from prison by an angel! Peter then went to the house where the people were praying for his release. Rhonda was so excited to hear Peter's voice through the door that she failed to open it. She disrupted the prayer meeting by shouting, "Peter is here!" The people told her that she was out of her mind: "...it is Peter's angel!" It was easier for them to believe that it was Peter's angel than to believe that God delivered Peter from prison!

The point is—angelic visitations were commonplace at that time. The day is coming when angelic manifestations and encounters will be commonplace, just like in the Book of Acts.

One of the most exciting aspects of this book is to realize that you are not alone. Angels are there to assist you in fulfilling the call of God on your life, and walking in the destiny that the Lord has ordained for you. Angels will co-labor with you as you step out to do the works of Jesus.

Dancing With Angels 1 will clear up misconceptions you may have about the ministries and functions of angels on the earth today. It is also full of practical information to help you experience the angelic realm.

GARY OATES
Author, *Open My Eyes, Lord*
International Conference Speaker

Kevin Basconi's new book *Dancing With Angels 1: How to Work With the Angels in Your Life* is quite compelling. It was spiritually encouraging, uplifting, and probably one of the best books I've read for a very long time. It is written extremely well and it is easy to read. In fact I couldn't put it down! It is full of useful information to help the reader understand angelic ministry, and I loved the testimonies of angelic visitations. *Dancing With Angels 1* is also full of useful insights and was extremely inspirational to my faith in God. I would highly recommend that every pastor read this book and put into action the scriptural principles that Kevin outlines. I whole heartily recommend *Dancing With Angels 1*.

Dr. Jonathan Tan
London, England

Wow! I have just read *Dancing With Angels 1* written by Kevin Basconi, and I highly recommend it. Kevin and his wife Kathy are people who have allowed the Lord to mold themselves into real vessels for His use. Throughout my nine years of working with King of Glory Ministries International here in Africa, my eyes have seen God's tremendous glory, and many, many miracles and healings in Kevin's ministry. Kevin is a man whose inner focus is on the Lord Jesus Himself. He has no other desire than to deliver the Word of God to hungry people around the world. His book gives great insight into what the Lord intends to do in the lives of many people worldwide. It is full of wisdom, knowledge, and revelation, and it contains much information about how anyone can work with God's angels in ministry and in all parts of life. Once you start reading *Dancing With Angels 1,* you can't put it down. I have personally benefited from this book as my understanding of the areas and ways that angels can work with me has expanded. Kevin has practically experienced what he says about working with God's angels. In 2006 I was with him here in Uganda, and in the same room on the night that we experienced a powerful angelic visitation together at the Imperial Botanical Beach Hotel in Kampala. Uganda. I realized that God has given Kevin a special kind of grace and faith to work with angels. As you read *Dancing With Angels 1*, allow the fire of God through its message to take you to a new level of working with the angels in your life too.

ZENOBIUS ISAYA, Bishop, Lake Victoria Zone
and Senior Pastor, Philadelphia Gospel Assembly
Mwanza, Tanzania

From the first time I met Kevin and Kathy, I was convinced that they were people of pure passion for the Lord and His Kingdom. I watched as they made sacrifices to reach those in dark and isolated regions of the world. I watched as they cared for the orphans and the poor. They are familiar with the angelic and the supernatural for sure, but more than that, they are friends of God, for they love what He loves.

PATRICIA KING
XPmedia.com

In the book *Dancing With Angels 1*, Kevin Basconi presents an inspirational, faith-building, and practical explanation of how ordinary believers can cooperate with and even release, or "loose," the ministry of angels to accomplish the will of God. He clearly shows how living with an awareness of the supernatural should be normal Christianity and not some paranormal activity. Based on the Scriptures, which are expounded upon throughout the book, Kevin helps believers properly discern the angelic ministry and activity that is currently taking place around all of us.

Furthermore, the book is filled with his personal testimonies of how he has grown to understand how angels are at work and how working with them dramatically increases our ability to accomplish God's will. Kevin's personal experiences and the testimonies of angelic visitations serve as faith builders and propel the reader to seek God more earnestly for the discernment needed to live in the reality of this angelic awareness and cooperation.

The book is also a great tool and guide that can prepare the Church to live in the times of the harvest and rapidly approaching healing revivals. Furthermore, the author stresses the necessity of proving any supernatural experience with the truths of the Bible. In this way, Kevin helps to keep the reader Word based. The book does not glorify angelic ministry, but explains their operation in the earth and how they, along with believers, can exalt Jesus as King and advance His Kingdom. I highly recommend this book!

DAVID WHITE, Senior Pastor
MorningStar Fellowship Church
Moravian Falls, NC

It is my pleasure to recommend this book, *Dancing With Angels 1*, by my friend Kevin Basconi. Kevin and his wife Kathy are the founders and directors of King of Glory Ministries. I was the Basconi's pastor for nearly five years and have been a member of King of Glory Ministries International's Board of Directors since 2004. They are anointed to proclaim the Gospel and dedicated to see Kingdom expansion. But their ministry is more than just words. It is marked by signs, wonders, and healings! There is a demonstration of the power of God! Their ministry is punctuated by the supernatural! These two echo the words of Isaiah 8:18, *"...We are for signs and wonders..."*

But how do all these miracles take place? The short answer is, we pray, and the Father answers. But He does so by sending angelic help to assist us whenever and in whatever way is needed! They are messengers of God, sent out to carry out His will (see Ps. 103:21). Kevin has learned, experienced, and shown how important angelic activity is in order to carry out God's plans and purposes.

This book will enlighten you to the work of angels. Kevin takes Scriptures that emphasize the ministry of angels and combines them with firsthand accounts of powerful angelic intervention. I have been with Kevin when these messengers from God show up, commissioned to bring healing, salvation, and miracles. Their interactive ministry is a reality! Hebrews 1:14 says that they are *"ministering spirits sent forth to minister for those who will inherit salvation...."* Not only do they minister *to* us, but also *for* us. Kevin is emphatic that they are fellow ministers, and while we need them, they are not to be worshiped...but respected and appreciated.

As you read this book, you will receive insights from the Word as to their purpose, power, and proximity to us. You will better understand the various types of angels and their function. You will become reflective as you think back to instances where they assisted you while you were completely unaware of their activity. You will gain new insights as to how they help and also how much we need their help. You will see, as the end of the ages approaches, that the role of angels will be even more essential. There will be a global revival with billions ushered into the Kingdom of God!

Angels will have a pivotal role in seeing the Father's plan to save the masses carried out.

There is much confusion and controversy pertaining to the angelic. This book will be a help to you. God bless you as you read and enjoy *Dancing With Angels 1!*

ALAN KOCH, founder and senior pastor
Christ Triumphant Church

I was overwhelmed as I began to read the new book *Dancing With Angels 1: How to Work With the Angels in Your Life.* I was sensing a strong presence of the Lord, and the anointing of the Holy Spirit as I read the testimonies of angelic visitations. I believe that the Lord's hand is working through this book, and that God's hand is upon the material in the book. I began to experience a hunger for more of God and all of His Kingdom as I read the book to the end. I am now sure that His desire is to open the eyes of the heart and to allow us to receive divine revelation and encounters with the Lord. We need more books like this; it's a journey into how we can work and cooperate with our Lord, Holy Spirit, and God's angels. This book is a very important resource for our spiritual growth, our lives, and even our ministries. *Dancing With Angels 1* is truly a gift from God for His people in these last days. It is a very timely book, and I highly recommend that everyone read this book, no matter how long they have been serving the Lord.

PASTOR PER ALTSVED
Christian Center
Stockholm, Sweden

Contents

ANGELS AND YOU

ARE ANGELS REAL?

Do angels actually intervene in the lives of ordinary people today? Or are they just a fantasy dreamed up by some Hollywood script writers for movies like Frank Capra's classic 1946 film, *It's a Wonderful Life?* Are angels like Clarence—or Dudley, from the 1947 movie, *The Bishop's Wife*—actually sent from Heaven to answer our prayers, release favor, revelation, supernatural provision, and spiritual experiences in the lives of people today? The answer is absolutely yes! In fact, these two classic movies are elegant prophetic pictures of how angelic ministry will begin to increase in the lives of people at this hour. The Bible tells us that angels are our fellow servants who are sent to help people (see Rev. 19:10; Heb. 1:14).

From the very beginning of my walk with Jesus, the supernatural aspects of the Lord have been evident in my life.

Angelic ministry impacts my wife and me on a regular basis. The Lord has commissioned angels to assist in the supernatural release of our calling and ministry. Angels are involved in many aspects of our lives. We embrace the activities of angels in our daily lives. You can too!

Because I have experienced supernatural encounters from the very inception of my Christian walk, I did not question the mystical aspects of the Kingdom of Heaven. I had not been "brought up" in the Church and had not been indoctrinated to believe that supernatural experiences were not intended to be a normal part of walking with Jesus today. After I had been saved a short time, I had been praying and asking the Lord what I was to do. The Lord explained to me how I could activate or "loose" angels to work on my behalf and for the benefit of others. Through the unfathomable work of the Holy Spirit, I just "knew" that God had a purpose for me. I began to ask Jesus about this on a daily basis.

Soon I began to experience visions, or what some call "third heaven" encounters. Even as a babe in Christ I would embrace these phenomena; I simply thought these kinds of experiences were supposed to be normal as a Christian. In one such vision I "saw" Jesus clearly in the spirit. He was calling me to draw closer to Him. Jesus was holding out His arms invitingly, and welcoming me to come into His presence. In my mind I had a decision to make. Either I would go to Jesus, or I would dismiss this vision and continue to pray to Him in my little prayer closet. I chose to go to Him. Immediately I sensed that I was being catapulted through time and space. A minute later I found myself in the very presence of Jesus Christ.

As Jesus wrapped His arms around me, I was overcome by the knowledge of the powerful love He has for me. Jesus said that He was going to tell me who I was. This of course was an answer to my ongoing prayers. Jesus said, "Kevin, I am calling you to be an artist, an author, and evangelist." Those words penetrated to the very depth and fiber of my being. The Lord held me for a long time, and I wept uncontrollably in His arms of love. When I stepped back from the Lord, I saw that He was flanked by four strong angels. These enchanting creatures seemed to be overjoyed that I was in the very presence of Jesus. The angels welcomed me as they smiled at me with assurance.

Jesus moved His right hand in a sweeping motion indicating the four angels that were present. He said, "Today I am appointing these angels to your ministry." I was a new believer. This statement baffled me, as I had no ministry. Just as quickly as it began, the experience was over. However, the feeling of Christ's supernatural love and presence rested upon me for days after that encounter. When the vision ended, I found myself back in my prayer closet weeping greatly. For several months, I continued to weep every time this event came into my mind.

A few days later, as I was praying, I "saw" Jesus again. He was requesting me to come to Him for a second time. I was ready to go without hesitation. I experienced the same sensation of being "launched" and could feel my spirit being "sucked out" of my body. I came to rest in the very presence of Jesus, and He was flanked by the same four angels. I fell to my knees and began to weep once again as I felt the power of His unconditional love. Two of the angels moved to my side and helped me to stand. Then Jesus looked deeply and lovingly into my eyes. Jesus placed His nail-scarred hands upon my shoulders. He told me that He was releasing the first of the four angels to me at that moment. My mind raced as I wondered what it meant to have an angel given to me. The Lord told me this angel's name and his function or anointing. The Lord also explained to me how people can activate angels to work on their behalf and for the benefit of others. Angels are empowered by the Lord to release provision and protection. You also have angels assigned to you with similar abilities.

Since these encounters, I have never doubted the existence of the Lord's angelic beings nor their constant intervention in my life. The Lord has frequently released me to utilize this particular angel throughout the years. We will look at many detailed examples of this angel's ministry in the coming pages. As a new Christian, I experienced the reality of angelic ministry firsthand. I have personally experienced how angels can impact our lives and the environment around people. As time has passed, the Lord has indeed assigned other angels to Kathy and me. We have also become more knowledgeable concerning the manner in which angels work in the lives of people. I will share some of those hidden mysteries with you in this book.

God has enabled Kathy and me to travel and minister extensively throughout the world preaching the Gospel of Jesus Christ. This was made possible through the Lord's angelic help. To date, we have visited six continents and 22 nations sharing the Gospel of the Kingdom. We have constantly been accompanied by the Lord's angels as we "go with the Gospel." Many people have seen these angels, and we have included their testimonies in this book. Angels are very active on the earth in our day, energetically involved in the lives of average people from every walk of life.

SUPERNATURAL ACTIVITY TODAY

Many people walk in a remarkable level of supernatural activity today. Throughout the Bible, there are accounts of angelic activity. Miracles, signs, wonders, and angelic encounters are also common with many folks. Certainly, the plethora of activity and visitations of angels did not stop with the Book of Acts. As Paul says in First Corinthians, our eyes have not seen, nor our ears heard, nor has it dawned upon our hearts the extraordinary things which God has prepared for those who love Him. The eyes of the Lord are actively seeking people that He can use to release angelic ministry right now! (See First Corinthians 2:9 and Second Chronicles 16:9.)

We are entering into a season, or appointed time, in which we need to lay down our personal agendas. It is imperative that we begin to demonstrate the Gospel of the Kingdom. An important aspect of this demonstration will be manifesting the Kingdom of God the same way Jesus did. One of the many tools the Lord has given us to release His power and manifest His Kingdom is angelic ministry. The Lord is doing glorious things in the earth today. Jesus taught us to pray for the Father's will to be done on earth as it is in Heaven (see Matt. 6:9-10). Jesus instructed people to invite the realm of Heaven to come to earth as we pray. The Bible clearly teaches us that a myriad of angels populate the realms of Heaven.

We have an open invitation to ask the Father to employ this unimaginably vast number of angels to work on our behalf.

The Lord has commissioned and is continuously releasing armies of angels that can help you in this hour. We live in the most exciting time in history. It is possible for ordinary men, women, and children to experience biblical-type encounters with angels. You can learn how to initiate and set angelic help in motion in your life and circumstances, too. God *is* sending angels to minister to people today. Encountering and working with angels should be normal and not a fearful, "spooky" affair.

RELEASING ANGELS

There are countless ways that the Lord releases angels today. The veil between the heavens and earth is thin, fragile, and more transparent than at any time in history. As the triumphant return of Christ approaches, the degree of supernatural activity of Elohim, the Creator of Heaven and earth, will dramatically increase—including the ministry and visitations of angels into our realm. Like it or not, God created angels, and they are still on the job throughout the earth. Angels were created by God and for His purposes. We should embrace His purposes *and* His angelic servants. God has angels who are assigned and ready to work in your life (see Col. 1:16).

Although this book was actually written in a short amount of time (see the Epilogue), it was tenderly birthed over the last nine years. During that time, I sought the Lord diligently about the angelic encounters I was experiencing. I have come to a conclusion as I have fasted, prayed, and researched the Scriptures concerning angels—it has always been God's plan to allow His sons and daughters to see, interact, experience, and work with angels. The Lord has called everyone to be aware of His spiritual Kingdom. Anyone can experience the supernatural realm where angels dwell. Angelic encounters and visitations should be a normal part of your life too. Several easy ways are outlined to help you access this realm and activate the angels in your life.

As my wife and I have traveled around the world, I have discovered that many ordinary people have regular experiences with angels. Those people simply have childlike faith and believe that they can encounter angels. They entertain angels, expecting them to materialize and impact their everyday lives. You can too. As a matter of fact, angels are actually extremely eager to interact with us. The Lord has shown me on numerous occasions that angels are eagerly awaiting our invitations and orders to send them on "missions of mercy."

I have witnessed the excitement of angels as they have been released in both the spirit and in the natural realm. Every time the angels are liberated to impact and work in this realm, they become exuberant and enthusiastic. This is a spiritual principle that the Lord has ordained for you; the Lord wants you to put His created beings to work! As we have developed friendships worldwide, I have seen how ordinary people have hungered to know more about angelic ministry. As we have shared these spiritual principles concerning angelic ministry, we have seen people grow and mature in this area. We have seen them empowered by the Lord to initiate angelic ministry in their own lives.

These are just ordinary people with whom we share these experiences. They are not well-known "superstars" of faith. In fact, I believe that the Lord would prefer it this way. The Father would prefer that ordinary people orchestrate extraordinary demonstrations of His Kingdom. There are many inspiring testimonies that give me great hope to believe that angels and their help are available to all of us. God has assigned angels to help regular folk minister and demonstrate His Kingdom. Scripture should be enough to give us all the hope and faith we need to believe we can experience angelic intervention in our lives. (See Revelation 14:6-7; 22:16; and Matthew 13:39.)

ANGELS ORDAINED TO HELP AND PROTECT

Scripture illustrates that God has ordained angels to help and protect you. Every believer is promised angelic help in their daily lives. We have seen these promises executed time and time again in our own lives; we have also witnessed how God has utilized angels to meet the needs of others throughout the earth. It is the very nature of the Lord to help meet our needs through angelic intervention and ministry (see Ps. 91:11-12; Heb. 1:14). When we graduate and put off this "earth suit" (die), we will all be astonished at the incredibly high level of angelic activity that constantly surrounded our everyday lives. We are going to look at many "normal angelic encounters" that illustrate this fact. Angels are all around us. They are ready, willing, and able to help meet our simplest needs.

VISITATION OF JESUS IN 2002

In 2002, I experienced a powerful visitation of Jesus. We will examine this experience in great detail later, but during that encounter, the Lord began to speak to me about the "seer anointing." I had no knowledge of the "seer anointing," and told the Lord so. He instructed me to read First Samuel 9, and said that He would begin teaching me more about this gift of prophecy in the coming years. He told me to begin to pray and study the Scriptures concerning the seer anointing. I pondered this visitation and the Lord's instructions in my heart for over five years. In 2007, I experienced another vision in which the Lord showed me a prophetic picture of the imminent release of the "seer anointing" that is being emancipated from the realms of Heaven and released *en masse*.

We have stepped into that *kairos* moment and season. The Lord is activating "seers" throughout the earth. The Lord will raise up ordinary people who will begin to be endued and anointed with the seer gift. This will actually be a restoration of the gift of discerning of spirits, and many people will begin to have the ability to see the angels that are already busy working around each of us. We will also be given unction from the Holy One to activate and "loose" angels to accomplish tasks for God's Kingdom and purposes on earth at this hour. God will empower and equip ordinary people to see into the spirit and work with angels to impact their environment. This empowerment will be pivotal to usher in the approaching global healing revivals and outpourings of God's Spirit that will cover the earth (see 1 John 2:20; Matt. 16:19).

CHRIST JESUS, THE CORNERSTONE

Christ Jesus must be the absolute cornerstone of our faith. We must worship the Lord alone and seek His perfect plans for our lives. However, angels are also an essential part of God's Kingdom. Consider the possibility that the Lord may have every intention to use His angelic hosts to meet your needs in the coming days. As we enter into this new season, we must be open to God's perfect will. This book may well be a tool that can help you become more sensitive to the Lord of host's angelic realm. Remember that many have entertained angels unaware, as they have entertained strangers (see Heb. 13:2).

You will be encouraged as you consider the biblical principles and modern-day accounts of angels. Keep in mind that this is the first book of a trilogy. The second book will be titled, *Dancing With Angels 2: The Role of the Holy Spirit and Open Heavens in Activating Your Angelic Visitations*. This book will elaborate on the material that is outlined in this first book in much greater depth and detail. The third book of the trilogy will be called, *Dancing With Angels 3: Angels in the Realms of Heaven*. The third book will depict angelic visitations that I have experienced in the realms of Heaven, and in it I will also describe the appearance of Heaven and heavenly places. Throughout the trilogy we will continue to build on a solid biblical foundation, learning more about the reality of angelic ministry today as we go along. You will discover how angelic visitations and ministry can affect your life in this hour. We will investigate numerous testimonies of recent angelic visitations in the next two books as well. Remember that every testimony of an angelic visitation that you read in these three action-packed books is a potential prophetic word for you.

Perhaps you will also be ready to embrace angelic ministry. If you do, your life will never be the same. Relax, pray, and ask the Holy Spirit to guide you as you read the following chapters. You may discover and step into a greater understanding of God's angels, the Kingdom of Heaven, and its King where *"...eye has not seen and ear has not heard, and which have not entered the heart of man, all that God has prepared for those who love Him"* (1 Cor. 2:9 NASB).

We are not advocating any new doctrine or theology. Jesus Christ must be the absolute cornerstone and foundation of our faith in God. As such, we do have the more sure word of prophecy (see 2 Pet. 1:19), the standards that are laid out in the canon of Scripture that are to guide our faith. The Word of God clearly states that Jesus has given gifts to men (see Eph. 4:8). These gifts are released and orchestrated through the marvelous working of the precious Holy Spirit.

Let's keep these things in mind as we begin our adventure of faith, seeking to learn about the reality of angelic ministry today. My goal is to activate your faith with the objective of helping the Body of Christ grow into the fullness of the knowledge of the Son of God. You can operate in the seer anointing. You can grow and mature in all things into Him who is the head—Christ (see Eph. 4:15). Angelic ministry is only one very small aspect of Jesus' Kingdom.

Understanding more facts and spiritual principles concerning angelic ministry can help anyone walk in the fullness and complete victory that Jesus purchased for all on the Cross. This understanding will transform you into an overcomer who will live in revelation, fullness, prosperity, victory, and triumph. (See Ephesians 4:15 and Revelation 2:7,11,17,26; 3:5; 21:7.) However, Christ must be *the Cornerstone* of your faith.

Let's examine how Jesus perceived angels and angelic ministry during His earthly life and ministry; then we will begin to look at modern-day testimonies of angelic encounters.

Chapter 1

JESUS, OUR ROLE MODEL

Earlier I shared how I embraced the supernatural as a new believer. As a result, I immediately began to encounter the angelic realm. I was aware of the fact that the Lord was utilizing angels to impact my life. It dawned on me that Jesus is in fact the Lord of hosts, the angelic hosts of Heaven. Angels are at His beck and call (see Ps. 24:10). As time passed, I began to encounter angels on a regular basis. I first began to *hear* angels; later I experienced the *touch* of angels. I also realized that when angels were present, they affected the natural world around me. This manifested as fragrances and also "glimpses" into the spirit as I would see "flashes" of light and simply have a "knowing" that angels were close by.

By embracing and entertaining angels, along with these associated phenomena, I exercised my spiritual senses by reason of use. This practice helped me to massage my ability to perceive and recognize angelic activity (see Heb. 5:14).

Later the Lord began to teach me how to interact with angels, and I began to see that angels impact the realm of earth in many ways. Angels work in symphony with the Holy Spirit and His gifts. Angels are sometimes discharged to empower ordinary people to operate in the gifts of the Spirit. Angels worked with Jesus Christ in a similar fashion as He walked and ministered on earth.

Jesus embraced angelic ministry from the very beginning of His earthly life to the very end of His earthly life. The angel Gabriel announced the very birth of Jesus Christ (see Luke 1:19,26). We also know that angels ministered to Jesus in the desert after He was tempted by the devil (see Matt. 4:11; Mark 1:13). Angels ministered to Jesus the night before He was crucified (see Luke 22:43). Angels were present at the Lord's resurrection (see Mark 16:5; Luke 24:4). Angels were also present at His ascension (see Acts 1:10-11). Angels ministered to Christ Jesus numerous times while He walked the earth as an ordinary man according to the Scriptures. The Scriptures also tell us in John 21:25 that *"there are also many other things that Jesus did, which if they were written one by one, I suppose that even the world itself could not contain the books that would be written."* Angels continue to minister to Christ today.

Angels played an important role in the resurrection of Christ by giving the disciples a message with important direction and guidance. The Lord sent an angel to tell His followers that He was indeed risen and to meet Him in Galilee. Angels delivered the greatest news ever heard, *"He is risen."* When the women went to the tomb, they experienced an angelic visitation. The angel quoted Jesus' words:

The angel answered and said to the women, "Do not be afraid, for I know that you seek Jesus who was crucified. He is not here; for He is risen, as He said. Come, see the place where the Lord lay. And go quickly and tell His disciples that He is risen from the dead, and indeed He is going before you into Galilee; there you will see Him..." (Matthew 28:5-7).

These Scriptures prove that the angels were aware of the things that Jesus preached. Angels may have recorded the ministry and words of Jesus Christ as He taught, spoke, and prophesied about His destiny on the Cross of Calvary. Angels are used in this manner in the lives of ordinary people today as well.

Jesus embraced the ministry of angels. The Lord is our role model who has given us an example to follow. There have been times over the last several years when I have personally observed how Jesus interacts with angels and also how angels interact with Jesus. Angels work under the command of Christ. Observing how the angels are obedient to quickly perform the Lord's every desire has opened my understanding to this spiritual dynamic.

We have the authority to employ our angelic friends and fellow servants of Jesus. When we are instructed to do so by the Spirit of God, we can activate angels to accomplish "missions" on earth, and also in the heavens. Many people have allowed the knowledge of our place and authority in God's Kingdom to be stolen from us. As you read the testimonies in the coming pages, please keep an open mind and remember that the testimony of Jesus can be the spirit of prophecy for your life.

ANGELIC MINISTRY IN THE LIFE OF CHRIST

I have had numerous visitations of Christ and it has been my experience that angels always accompany the resurrected Lord Jesus into the realms of earth today. The Scriptures also reveal that angels were employed to minister to Jesus. They certainly strengthened the Lord in His time of need on more than one occasion. It appears the angels ministered to the Lord Jesus as a result of His prayers. As Jesus prayed to His Father, He responded by releasing angels to minister to Jesus' needs (see Luke 22:43).

Angels ministered to Jesus in the beginning of His ministry. After the Lord was filled with the Holy Spirit, He was led into the wilderness and fasted for 40 days (see Matt. 4:1-2). During that time, the enemy tempted Jesus with the pride of life, the lust of the flesh, and the lust of the eyes. Jesus battled the deceiver with the Sword of the Spirit, the Word of God. Jesus successfully withstood the devil. The Lord fasted 40 days and 40 nights and grew very hungry. The Lord experienced angelic encounters during this period of His life, and the angels ministered to Jesus.

We read in Mark 1:13, *"He was there in the wilderness forty days, tempted by Satan, and was with the wild beasts; and the angels ministered to Him."* Did Jesus pray and release those angels? Did the angels actually minister to Jesus by giving Him some food? The Scriptures do not clearly spell this out, but it would seem logical that since Jesus was alone in the desert the angels ministered to Him by feeding Him. I have had an angel provide strawberry jam to me!

Jesus Christ taught and prophesied that He had all authority to employ angels to help Him while He ministered on the earth. (See Matthew 26:53; 16:27; 24:31; Luke 9:26.) The Lord also gave ordinary people all power and supernatural authority to delegate angelic ministry. We have the authority or jurisdiction to pray to our Father in the name of Jesus Christ and ask the Lord to release a multitude of angels. Jesus has commanded us to do the same type of works that He did (see John 14:12-14). One tool that we have been given to accomplish this is angelic ministry (see Matt. 18:18-20).

Jesus has a great deal of revelation about angelic ministry. Jesus was aware that He could employ angelic ministry to accomplish His work. You can too. The Bible is very clear about this matter. There are dozens of Scriptures in the first four Gospels alone in which angels are mentioned in relation to Christ's birth, ministry, or life. There are over two dozen examples in the harmony of the Gospels in which Jesus refers to, prophesies, or teaches about angelic ministry and the duties of angels. A large portion of the Book of Revelation was dictated to the apostle John on the island of Patmos by Jesus Christ's angel.

Clearly, it would seem that not only does the Messiah believe in and activate angelic ministry, but that the Lord still employs angels to relate His wishes to us today. Perhaps this should be indicative of our lives too. Jesus uses His angel to relate His last recorded words in the Bible to us. I believe that the Scriptures show plainly that Jesus will continue to employ angels to complete His end-time mandates upon the earth. Look at Revelation 1:1: *"The Revelation of Jesus Christ, which God gave Him to show His servants—things which must shortly take place. And He sent and signified it by **His angel** to His servant John."*

On the night that He was to be betrayed and start the journey that would eventually lead to His death on the Cross of Calvary, Jesus referred to His ability to initiate angelic ministry. Jesus said, *"Do you think that I cannot now pray to My Father, and He will provide Me with more than twelve legions of angels?"* (Matt. 26:53). In this passage, Jesus illustrated one of the most important keys to releasing angelic ministry. He tells us that He has the authority to *"pray to My Father."* The Lord clearly states that He had at that moment of need an estimated 72,000 angels who could come to His aid. We are entering into a season when the Lord will begin to empower ordinary people to carry this kind of authority and power.

Jesus also refers to His triumphant return as one that will be notable by the multitude of angels that will accompany Him (see Matt. 24:30-31). Jesus prophesies that His return will be accompanied by "His angels" who will be employed to gather His elect from the corners of the earth. The apostle John spoke of a number that was ten thousand by ten thousand in reference to the number of angels that he saw in Heaven. Many theologians believe that this indicates an innumerable host of angels. Jesus plans to return with a number of angels too large for our human minds to comprehend. Jesus knows about angelic ministry.

JESUS TAUGHT ABOUT ANGELS

Jesus prophesied about the abundance of angelic ministry in our day. This prophecy was given over 2,000 years ago. We are entering into the season when this prophetic word will begin to manifest in the lives of ordinary people. Jesus told Nathanael, *"Most assuredly, I say to you, hereafter you shall see heaven open, and the angels of God ascending and descending upon the Son of Man"* (John 1:51). This is a clear picture of God's preordained plan for humankind. We have entered that *kairos* time today. Jesus prophesied that the heavens would open. This was one of Christ's most important objectives of His earthly ministry. Jesus came to restore the open heavens back over mankind, and thereby reunite the Creator to the creature, mankind. Today the heavens are open, and the angels of God are becoming very active in the realms of earth. God created a spiritual realm or dwelling place, and He also created a temporal, earthly realm. This is the nature of creation and is further illustrated in Genesis 1. The Lord divided the heavens or spiritual realm from the terrestrial or temporal realm. Genesis 2:4 also illustrates the separation of the earthly realm and the spiritual realm. The passage in Genesis 2 also refers to several heavens, but for the sake of this study we will only speak in terms of the heavens and the earth, although some theologians believe there could be as many as 21 levels of heaven, hence the terms, *third heaven* and *seventh heaven*.

The angels of God are becoming very active in the lives of ordinary people who are friends of God. What a time to be alive! Jesus has given us a very clear pattern to follow;

He modeled how to implement angelic ministry. In John 5:19-20, Jesus tells us that obedience is crucial: *"...Most assuredly, I say to you, the Son can do nothing of Himself, but what He sees the Father do; for whatever He does, the Son also does in like manner. For the Father loves the Son...."* Jesus only sought to implement those things on earth that He "saw" His Father doing. Jesus was a seer. The Lord was obedient, and lived His life out of the total obedience or unction of the Holy Spirit. Jesus is now releasing the seer anointing to people throughout the earth.

Jesus instructed us to pray according to the will of His Father and "loose" in Heaven and "bind on earth." We see this illustrated for us in Matthew 16:19: *"And I will give you the keys of the kingdom of heaven, and whatever you bind on earth will be bound in heaven, and whatever you loose on earth will be loosed in heaven."* We have been given authority to "loose angelic ministry." We have also been instructed to release the Kingdom of Heaven upon the earth as we pray (see Luke 11:2; Matt. 6:10).

As we prepare our hearts and seek the Kingdom of Heaven, many people will encounter heavenly visitors, much as the women did, when we begin to see the resurrected Christ. Through angelic ministry, many people will begin to receive divine direction and revelation for their lives and their own personal safety in this hour. Visitations of angels will soon become much more frequent and commonplace. It is certain that the Lord Jesus Himself believed in the ministry of angels and was aware of what method and manner was needed to activate angelic ministry. Jesus also embraced the ministry of angels as they played a key role throughout His life and ministry. The Lord has given you and me a wonderful example to follow. We can welcome and employ angelic ministry just like Jesus Christ.

Christ has shown us that He embraced angelic ministry from before the time that He was conceived right up to His ascension. I can assure you that Jesus still embraces angelic ministry today. The Lord promised to return with His angels in the future. Look at Matthew 25:31: *"When the Son of Man comes in His glory, and all the holy angels with Him, then He will sit on the throne of His glory."* It is my opinion that Jesus Christ has given us a very clear pattern to emulate in relationship to angels and angelic ministry! (See 1 Peter 2:21.)

Jesus is the perfect representation of our heavenly Father. The Lord perfectly represents the covenantal names of God and manifested those attributes in His life on earth (see John 14:7-12). Jesus walked with nobility and humility. We need to emulate Jesus in these attitudes. One method that the Lord uses to manifest His covenantal nature today is angelic intervention in the lives of ordinary people.

We have allowed the enemy of our souls to steal a wonderful, powerful, and important facet of our heritage—angelic ministry. Angelic encounters should not be spooky or fearful. We have allowed fear of the unknown to paralyze us and limit our ability to operate in the realms of the supernatural. We are stepping into a God-ordained moment when the Lord will return our ability to understand how to interact with the spiritual realm. One way that the Spirit of God will accomplish this is by restoring the gift of discerning of spirits to individuals. God is beginning to raise up people who "see" into the spiritual realm or operate in the seer anointing.

In the coming pages, I will share many testimonies about how angels minister to people on the earth today. I have learned through many experiences with angelic ministry that Jesus' angels also walk in humility and nobility. The amount of angelic activity in the life of the resurrected Savior has increased drastically compared to His earthly life. Why? Because the number of angels in the heavens surrounding the risen Savior are innumerable.

However, the interaction that Jesus had with angels during His life on earth was tremendous. Since He has given us an example to follow, we should also enjoy a tremendous amount of angelic interaction in our lives. Angelic encounters should be a normal part of our Christian walk. Now let's investigate modern testimonies of angelic encounters and how angels work.

THE REALITY OF ANGELIC MINISTRY TODAY

A RETROSPECTIVE LOOK

Let's begin by taking a retrospective look at some of the angelic encounters that we have experienced. This will continue to build our foundation and your faith. I have worked to the best of my ability to record all of these events as accurately as possible. However, in the sphere of the supernatural, it can be difficult to translate a spiritual experience into the natural realm. I am limited by my human words and mind. In addition, I am relating events that occurred some years ago. Sometimes I have notes to refer to, but at other times I am depending on memory and the Holy Spirit to help me. Unless specifically asked to keep identities anonymous, I have sought to be as straightforward as possible in this writing by including the actual names of the places and people involved.

The subsequent series of testimonies illustrates several keys that will help you activate your ability to perceive angels in your life. I have found over the years that as I practice these spiritual exercises, my ability to see angels multiplies (see Heb. 5:14). Two of the most important keys are the combination of prayer and fasting. As you press into the Kingdom of God with these two keys, they seem to activate the ability to see and perceive angels. When you combine these two keys with a regimen of devotions and reading Scripture, the ability to see and perceive angels seems to flourish.

At times the Lord will require you to perform a certain task or what some call a "prophetic act." Often these acts will be something that will take you out of your comfort zone and will cost you greatly in one way or another. It is critical to be obedient to the Holy Spirit at that time.

It is also important to "entertain angels" and to simply ask the Lord to open your eyes to see the angels around you. We will look at these spiritual tools in greater detail later. However, you may wish to note how these keys are evident in the testimonies that follow. Remember, you can employ these simple keys and spiritual tools too. Implementing these simple spiritual tools can be pivotal to learning to work with God's angels.

Your Kingdom Come

Forty-seven days after I was born again and delivered from a 30-year drug addiction, the supernatural reality of God crashed into my life. I had been fasting intensely and praying for several weeks, asking Jesus to reveal Himself to me. On April 13, 2001, at 1:13 A.M., I had a visitation of God. I was awakened by the strong smell of frankincense. Suddenly an angel stepped into the room, and I heard an audible voice giving me divine instruction for evangelism. From that day forward, the aspects of our supernatural God have been manifesting in my life. I can point to that early morning as the beginning of my ability to perceive angelic activity. It was also the start of ministry in my life and laid the foundation for King of Glory Ministries International. Because of this angelic encounter, I began to reach out to the lost in my city through the King of Glory Music Festival. This free festival was held at the Sarah Creasy Metcalf Amphitheatre in Bluefield, Virginia. The festival was born as a direct result of the audible words that I heard the angel speak to me.

This encounter created a hunger for God in my life, and the Lord began to open the realms of the supernatural to me. Because of this hunger for God, I fasted and read the Bible voraciously. I began to experience the realm of angels as the fragrance of the Lord invaded my time and space. I would sense angelic activity near me on a regular basis. The grace and favor of the Lord manifested in my life. Many people began to recognize that God was answering my prayers in supernatural ways.

Natural Miracles

Natural miracles became common in my life. One of the natural miracles that occurred during this season was the donation of a large banner for the festival. The banner reads "Jesus King of Glory" in bold red letters. On the night of August 22, 2001, I took the new banner to the church and asked Pastor Tim if we could pray over it and anoint it with oil.

Standing on the left end of the banner, I unrolled the material out in front of the altar, and the entire congregation gathered around it and prayed. The pastor anointed it with oil. I closed my eyes and began to pray in the Spirit. Suddenly, a familiar fragrance of frankincense enveloped me, and I felt a pair of very gentle, warm hands softly land upon my shoulders. Immediately I was touched by the Holy Spirit.

I felt the sensation of warm oil being poured over my head. The oil seemed to flow along my back and chest. The fragrance of the Lord began to fill my nose. The anointing of the Lord began to course through my weary body. I remember wondering, *Who on earth is praying for me?* I do not actually know how long I spent on my knees with my hands on the banner praying in the Holy Spirit, but those heavenly hands remained upon my shoulders the whole time. When I finally opened my eyes and looked up, it seemed that the other people in the church had ceased praying long ago. I was surprised to see that everyone was now seated back in their pews.

I was still on my knees with my hands on the left edge of the new banner. I could still tangibly feel those soft, anointed, and warm hands on my back. I remember thinking, *Well, at least someone stood beside me while I prayed.* I stood up to thank that "person" and turned around. I was astonished to find there was not a soul there. There was no one within 20 feet of me. I was totally flabbergasted! Just a split second before, I felt the hands upon my back and heard a soft voice praying in tongues along with me. The voice was very real and close by my left ear. I rolled up the banner and sauntered back to my seat, powerfully touched by the Holy Spirit. The wonderful anointing and the abiding presence of Jesus that I experienced that night did not lift from me for many days! And the banner, as of this writing, has been witness to over 70,000 salvations.

After this angelic encounter, the amount of grace and favor that was upon my life exploded. I went home that night, fell into my tiny prayer closet, and began to weep and thank the Lord for the encounter. I knew the Father had sent an angel to minister to me during the service. I asked Him why and what happened when I felt the oil running down my head and body. Immediately I was put in remembrance of the words that I had been praying while fasting for weeks: *"...Oh that You would bless me indeed...that Your hand would be with me..."* (1 Chron. 4:10).

God had sent an angel to place his hands on me! It is possible that the angel imparted an anointing and gift of grace upon my life. After that night I had a divine "knowing" that angels were real and that they were actually assigned to minister to and help me. I never once felt that angelic visitations were scary, spooky, or unnatural. Because I saw the ministry of angels in the Word of God, I accepted them without hesitation. I simply embraced angelic ministry with childlike faith.

After these initial encounters with the Kingdom of Heaven, I began to develop a desperate hunger for more of the Lord. Jesus initiated a metamorphosis in my life, and I pressed into a season of extended prayer and fasting. However, when the King of Glory Festival was over, the grace and favor that had been upon my life seemed to vanish. I was still experiencing the manifest presence of the Lord during times of prayer though. Occasionally the fragrance and anointing of God would fill my prayer room in the little house at 121 Beech Street, Bluefield, West Virginia. However, the frequency of the manifestations of God's presence had decreased greatly. I began to get desperate for God. In hindsight, I believe that the Lord orchestrated my thirst. I began to ask the Lord what He wanted me to do next.

DANCING ANGELS

During October 2001, the Lord began to speak to me about traveling to Newfoundland, Canada. I had no desire to go there, especially in the middle of the winter! At this time I was still concerned about my inability to "feel the Lord" and began to press into God all the more. At times I locked myself into the little house and fasted and prayed for up to seven days, or until the presence of God fell. After many confirmations in the spirit, I pooled all of my earthly wealth and made the trip to the great white North. The night before I was to depart, the Lord instructed me to "pray in tongues all the way to Newfoundland." Somehow through the grace of God I succeeded in praying in the Spirit for about 18 hours until I touched down in Canada.

In Springdale, Newfoundland, Canada, the Lord began instructing me to complete a series of prophetic actions. I attended an intercessory prayer meeting on Wednesday, November 21. We were interceding for an upcoming series of healing meetings. During this meeting, I began to "see" into the spirit. As the Lord opened my spiritual eyes, I incrementally saw the heavens open over Living Waters Ministries Church. In addition to this, I also began to hear angelic voices singing along with the worship team. At one point during the meeting, I saw a stream of golden oil pour out from Heaven and land on a certain spot in the sanctuary. At the leading of the Lord, I knelt upon that spot. The glory and anointing began to flow into and over my body. The sensation and anointing was very similar to what I experienced when the angel put his hands upon me the night of August 22, 2001.

As I knelt under the spot where the golden oil was beginning to pour onto the altar, I was praying earnestly. I could feel the liquid oil raining down on my body. I could sense and smell this heavenly oil as it rolled off my head. The Holy Spirit began to talk to me in a very clear and direct way that I had never experienced before. I collapsed onto the carpet in a pool of golden oil and laid there in the anointing of the Holy Spirit.

Then I sensed angels dancing all around the pool and me. I felt an angel as it brushed its wings across my face. I had a "knowing" that the angel was asking me to raise my hands into the air. When I raised my hands up to about two feet, the angel would push my hands back down with its strong, warm hands. I tried again, and when my hands were almost totally up, the angel tickled my nose with the feathers of its wings. I laughed, and my hands fell. The angel and I continued to interact in this fashion for nearly an hour. I did not actually see this angel, but the force and reality of its touch was very tangible. There was no doubt that I was interacting with a heavenly being. This experience was both refreshing and real.

SEEING IS BELIEVING

On Thursday, November 22, the healing meetings started; they would last through Sunday, the 25th. In these meetings God began to open my spiritual eyes beyond anything I could have ever imagined. On the first night of these meetings, I began to see an "open heaven" forming in the sanctuary. I could also hear and sense the activity of angels as the heavens continued to open up to a greater degree. On Friday, I began to see "bolts of light" shoot through the church, and again the stream of golden oil was flowing from the open heaven in a greater volume.

On Saturday night during the worship service, I began to see feathers falling around the church and again heard the voices of angels very clearly in the natural realm.

As the worship proceeded that evening, I began to feel the tangible and intense glory of God flood the room. I was worshiping Jesus with all of my heart near the front row. Suddenly I needed to open my eyes and look at the worship team. I was hearing dozens of singers accompanying the small worship team consisting of only five or six individuals. I was certain that angels were singing in unison with them. When I opened my eyes, I saw the source of the increased glory. Two in the worship team, Rose and Colleen, had one hand raised and one hand held a microphone as they were singing. When I glanced behind them, I saw a man adorned in a white robe standing there. His robe was immaculate.

It was whiter than any garment I have seen on earth and seemed to give off a translucent glow (see Matt. 17:2; Luke 24:4).

At first I shook my head and blinked my eyes, thinking that my eyes were playing a trick on me. When I opened them again, the angel was still there. I leaned forward and really strained my eyes for a good look. This magnificent angel was gazing right at me! He gave me a big smile, and then he winked at me! My mouth dropped open, and my eyes bulged out as every hair on my body stood on end! He continued to smile at me and look me over. Again I blinked my eyes and tried to shake off this vision that was crystal clear to me. Again when I opened my eyes, the angel was still there. He was still smiling at me and standing in a posture of attention and readiness. His robe seemed to emit a glow, and the material looked phosphorescent.

This heavenly visitor stood about 12 feet tall. The angel possessed a magnificent pair of beautiful white wings. He had long golden hair about shoulder length. His eyes were a bright piercing blue. He had a golden belt or sash around his waist. Upon the sash was a large two-edged sword with a heavy golden handle. On his wrists were ornate golden bands, and his feet were clad with golden sandals. He also carried a large golden shield that was of the finest workmanship. I watched this angel throughout the entire worship service. The angel looked at other individuals in the sanctuary from time to time. I was totally engrossed in observing every aspect of him. I was mesmerized by what I was witnessing. Every so often he would look at me and offer another smile.

OH, THAT YOU WOULD REND THE HEAVENS! THAT YOU WOULD COME DOWN! THE HEAVENS OPEN!

The momentum of these meetings continued to build. In desperation, I positioned my heart to encounter God. I continued to see the open heaven swirling in the sanctuary of Living Waters Ministries. I was still seeing feathers and bolts of lightning, and hearing dozens of angels singing along with the worship team. On Saturday evening, the open heaven had grown to about a 25-foot circumference. I was well able to see it with my natural eyes and continued to watch it spin over the church. I was praying and observing everything. I was lying prostrate on the floor unable to move my body. I could see, and I could hear, but was totally unable to move. It was as if I was glued to the floor. However, I kept my eyes focused on the open heaven that was swirling in the church.

I found myself in the same position on Sunday morning when a young man named Dean stood up to give his testimony about seeing Jesus in the Saturday evening service. When he began to share, I noticed that there was a flurry of activity around the edge of the open heaven that I was monitoring from my horizontal position on the floor. Dean became totally undone and was unable to speak about his experience. Several angels scurried to the edge and began to excitedly talk among themselves and point down at Dean. At first there were about six angels, and they were very keen to hear and see what was transpiring in the sanctuary. Soon a plethora of angels began to fill the circumference of the portal.

There appeared to be angels of all ages, shapes, and sizes. I saw several small angels that appeared to be young children. (Jesus Himself referred to these; see Matthew 18:10.) I also witnessed angels that appeared to be adults. There were also other smaller angels that were holding musical instruments. These instruments had the aspects of horns and trumpets, and others looked like flutes or reed instruments. There was a varied and vast assortment of angels represented in the small group of about 45 heavenly beings. I watched these angels for the remainder of the service. Soon I began to realize that the angels were aware of the fact that I could see them. Many of them began to point in my direction and speak to one another animatedly. This was fascinating.

God used the time I was in Newfoundland to open up my spirit and my spiritual eyes to a new dimension. The trip to Newfoundland prophetically represented a "new found land" for me in the realm of the spirit. I am sure that it was the grace of God that allowed me to begin to see angels. However, I would later discover that when I petitioned the Lord to "open my eyes" and other senses to perceive angelic activity, He was more than willing to do so. By implementing prayer and fasting, (especially praying in the Holy Spirit), combined with devotions, reading, and meditating upon the Scriptures, the ability to see and perceive angels seems to flourish. It is also important to be obedient to the Spirit of God in these times of seeking.

But—I was totally unprepared for what happened in the next meeting!

Chapter 3

JESUS AND THE ANGELS

On November 25 when the Sunday evening service opened, I checked for the spinning vortex that I had been seeing in the church. It was slowly rotating over the altar; it was only about 4 feet in diameter. When worship started, the "portal" began to spin more quickly and grew in size. Shortly, the opening had bloomed and was about 45 feet around. There were angelic voices falling from the heavens into the church. I closed my eyes and entered into the glory and worship of Jesus. When I checked the portal again, angels were positioned around the edge, talking among themselves. This was exciting!

Pastor Dave Mercer once again asked the young man, Dean, to give his testimony to the congregation about seeing Jesus. As Dean began to speak, there was another flurry of activity around the portal. Many angels began to peer down into the service and appeared quite anxious to hear Dean's words. There were dozens of angels around the perimeter of the opening. These heavenly beings were pointing and conversing avidly with one another.

Suddenly the large angel I had seen behind the worship team stepped up to the opening and looked at Dean. The glory of God greatly multiplied as he shouted something back over his shoulder. Then he motioned with his right arm. Immediately, the angels around the portal moved aside to clear a space. My eyes were drawn to the vacant area, and the glory of God greatly increased again. The anointing and power of God that was upon me at that moment was incredible. As Dean was speaking about seeing Jesus through tears of joy, the Lord appeared. Jesus stepped up to the edge of the portal. My eyes were transfixed upon the Messiah. I was totally undone in His presence and this supernatural saga that was unfolding before my eyes. The Lord held out His hands, and I watched in astonishment as Jesus began to rain down gemstones into the meeting. I saw what appeared to be diamonds, rubies, and pearls fall from the Lord's hands and bounce upon the churches floor.

JESUS DESCENDED INTO THE CHURCH

Jesus took one step with His left foot and descended into the church. As the Lord Jesus entered the sanctuary, the glory, anointing, and love of God became almost unbearable. Jesus walked over to Dean and placed His hands upon his shoulders as he spoke. Jesus then began to look around the church. He looked deeply into the individual hearts of the people for several moments. The Lord surveyed every person in the sanctuary, working from the right to the left. (See Psalm 44:21; Jeremiah 17:10; First Chronicles 28:9.)

I thought, *It doesn't get any better than this.* At that moment the Lord Christ Jesus turned and looked deeply into my eyes. Waves of God's love washed over me. I was totally undone. Then the Lord turned and walked over to me and stood over my prostrate body. I looked deeply into the eyes of God. They are the most beautiful eyes in the universe. For a fleeting moment I had the tiniest revelation of His endless love for me. Christ smiled broadly and gazed into my eyes and heart for several minutes. All I could do was to behold His glory. I was consumed by His perfect love and the passion He holds for me, and all of mankind.

Then Jesus spoke to me, "All authority has been given to Me in Heaven and on earth. Go and make disciples of all the nations; baptize them in the name of the Father and of the Son and of the Holy Spirit. Teach them to observe all things that I have commanded you; I will be with you always, everywhere you go. I will visit you and perform My good word toward you. You shall return to this place. My thoughts for you are thoughts of peace and not of evil, to give you a future and a hope. You will call upon Me and go and pray to Me, and I will listen to you. And you will seek Me and find Me when you search for Me with all your heart" (see Matt. 28:18-20; Jer. 29:10-14).

God continued to smile at me and looked intently into my eyes for another few minutes. I was unable to think. All I could do was breathe in His presence and enjoy His pure love for me. It also occurred to me that the fragrance that had manifested when the angels first visited me was also present—only the smell was much more concentrated. The heavenly aroma was more palatable than I had ever experienced it before. I could taste the fragrance of the Lord. It tasted like liquid roses and honey. The angels around the portal were focusing on the Lord as He ministered to me.

Suddenly I realized that Jesus wanted me to raise my left hand. I managed to move my left arm and hand. Later I thought that it may have been one reason that the angel was playing with my hands earlier. As I did so, Christ Jesus took my left hand into His nail-scarred hands. I could both see and feel the wounds on His hands. Gently the Lord Jesus blew upon my hand. It felt like warm oil ran down my arm. The Lord held my left hand in His hands for a moment, gazing lovingly into my eyes. Then He tenderly placed my left hand back upon my heart and stood up. Jesus smiled and lingered over me for several moments. Then Jesus turned again and walked back over to Dean. The Lord placed His hands upon his shoulders a second time, and then Jesus turned and ascended back into the heavenlies through the open heaven (see Acts 1:11).

I was unable to move and was totally undone by the presence and glory of God. When Jesus reached the portal, He simply stepped into the vacant section and disappeared into the heavens. My eyes were still transfixed upon the spot. Great streams of healing tears were pouring from my eyes. It seemed that I had experienced a cleansing of my spirit and soul.

I continued to watch the angelic host as they laughed, frolicked, and pointed down into the church. They were having a great time. However, I was no longer so astonished or mesmerized by their presence. All I could think about was the Lord and what He had commissioned me to do. The supernatural, unparalleled love Jesus carries deep within His heart for each of us is impossible for us to comprehend with our earthly minds. There are absolutely no words available in the English language that would allow me to relate to you accurately the unfathomable love that the Son of God has for you. For the next six months, the presence of the Holy Spirit was my constant companion. The Holy Spirit became so real to me that it seemed I was in constant communication with Him.

ANGELS AND THE BAPTISM OF FIRE

I purposed in my heart to travel to the city of St. John to attend the next two meetings in Newfoundland. The presence of the Holy Spirit had become so strong in my life that it was as if His shadow was with me at all times. The Lord was directing me to press into His Kingdom and continue to attend the revival meetings. This was way out of my comfort zone, but I knew that it was God's Spirit who was asking me to go. My friend and I arrived at the church in St. John just as the meeting began. I could sense the presence of angels. However, I was unable to see them in this service.

It was not until after 2 A.M. that I actually encountered the angels that early Monday morning. The way this encounter occurred was yet another learning experience for me. A wonderful couple, Rod and Wenda, had invited my friend and me to stay in their home near St. John. My room was well-appointed with a large king-size bed. Although in the natural I should have been physically exhausted, I was not. In fact I was exhilarated in the spirit and soon began to worship the Lord. It was good to be alone in the presence of the Holy Spirit again. It was just past 2 A.M. Soon I was praying, and the Lord directed me to begin to read out loud from Revelation 4. I read the passage once, and the Holy Spirit said, "Read it again." So I did. Then the Holy Spirit instructed me to read it out loud, and I did. I read this passage aloud over and over.

Suddenly, I felt the anointing and glory that I had experienced on the night of November 25 fill the room, and I heard a loud whistling sound. I looked up and saw a ball of fire falling from Heaven! This supernatural fireball was streaking from Heaven and was headed right at me! It was about 18 inches in diameter and was moving at the speed of sound! Before I had a chance to brace or even think, the ball of fire slammed into my belly.

At once I began to pray loudly in tongues. I had no control over my mouth. It was as if a river was flowing from the inner depths of my spirit. My body violently jerked as the fireball imploded within me. My legs and arms flew into the air! My trusty King James Bible flew across the room as the ball of fire struck my solar plexus! Perhaps this was the baptism of the Holy Ghost and fire? The fireball was assimilated into my spirit, soul, and body (see Matt. 3:11; Luke 3:16).

In an instant, my body was on fire, and I found myself hurtling through space. I looked down and saw my body jerking upon the bed and could hear myself praying in tongues as my spirit was sucked out of my body and through the roof of the house. I was launched out past the atmosphere of the earth. I could see the island of Newfoundland in the distance growing smaller below me. As I looked to my left, I saw that there was an angel who had taken me by my left hand and was carrying me into the spiritual realm. I was not fearful but only astonished. The angel did not speak to me but looked at me reassuringly. As we ascended higher, I could see the curvature of the earth below. I saw the sun as it began to rise in the East over Europe. Somehow I was given the revelation that I would be preaching there in the near future. It was an absolutely breathtaking sight. Shortly, the angel set me gently down in a broad place.

There were four other angels there, and they appeared to be expecting me. These were the same four angels that Jesus told me that He was assigning to me. This place was full of light, and the floor seemed to be made of a golden substance. The wonderful sounds of harps and violins filled the unimaginably clean air around Christ. I had sunk to my knees upon "landing." As I arose, I saw Jesus. He came directly to me and took me by the hand. The Lord then began telling me about my destiny. Soon I found myself walking with Jesus by the shore of a crystal-clear sea. Jesus took me from place to place, and He showed me events that are yet to come. After we had visited many places, we returned to the place where the first angel had "dropped me off." The other four angels were still there, and they seemed to be waiting for Christ's return.

When we arrived, the Lord began to speak to me about these angels. Jesus told me that He was assigning a second angel to me at that moment. Jesus told me the angel's name and what his ministry was to be. The other two angels were to be deployed to me in the future. This second angel was commissioned to help with releasing miracles and healings. I was given his name and told how to co-labor with the angel to help meet people's needs.

The Lord embraced me and bid me farewell. There were so many things that I longed to ask Him, but it was too late. I was being transported back through time and space by the first strong angel. I saw Earth below become larger. I saw Newfoundland and then Rob and Wenda's house. Suddenly I passed through the roof and was sucked back into my body. I was totally covered in sweat. The room was light; it was now 8:30 A.M. I estimated that I had been in the spirit for nearly six hours. I opened my mouth to say a prayer of thanks, and all that came out was tongues! I stayed in the room for another three hours or so and just pondered in my heart all that had transpired.

The Lord was certainly busy rearranging my ability to hear the Holy Spirit speaking to me and to completely trust Him. I felt that I was supposed to travel to Botwood for the last two meetings. I had little in the way of funds when I departed from Rob and Wenda's house and had not planned for a place to stay. I knew that the Lord would certainly provide all of our needs. We traveled through a heavy snow storm and arrived in Botwood just in time for the service. A beautiful Christian woman, Margaret, approached me and told me that the Holy Spirit had directed her to ask if we needed a place to stay! It was another answer to prayer, and I graciously accepted her offer.

When the service began, I was not surprised to hear the angelic hosts join with the worship team. In fact, several people in the church testified to hearing the angels. After the service, we traveled to Tim Horton's for a late dinner. We returned to Botwood to find Margaret waiting for us, and she kindly directed us to our separate rooms for the night. The Holy Spirit was still hovering very close to me, and as soon as the door closed behind my host, the Lord began to speak to me. I immediately began to pray and worship the Lord. Once again, the Lord had me begin reading from Revelation 4. It was about 3:30 A.M. when I fell into a peaceful sleep praying in the Spirit.

I awoke to the sound of the Lord's voice speaking to me. "Kevin, get up; it's time to go to work." I opened my eyes and looked around the room. My mind began to race. I looked at the clock, and it was just 5:00 A.M. I had only been asleep for a short while.

I sleepily said, "Lord, what could you possibly want me to do at this hour?"

"Walk downstairs and prophesy to Margaret," He said.

I protested, "Lord, I don't even know Margaret."

He said, "Don't worry. I know her. Just say what I tell you to say."

"But Lord, It's only 5 A.M., and nobody is awake at 5 A.M."

He answered, "Margaret is awake. She is in the kitchen. She is praying and having tea and a scone. Go to her now."

In my natural mind this seemed totally insane! Me? Prophesy?

Suddenly the anointing and presence of the Lord intensified, and I found myself dressed. The next thing I knew I was walking down the hallway toward the stairs. All at once, there was a still, small voice speaking into my left ear. I was being told many things about Margaret. I was hearing the secrets of her heart. When I walked into the kitchen, she was there. She was having tea and a scone. I asked her what she was doing, and she told me that she was praying.

PROPHESYING ABOUT ANGELS

I said, "Margaret, I think God wants me to tell you something!"

Her eyes grew as big as saucers as I launched into a litany of words about angels. I was as shocked as she was! I was able to speak in great detail about angels to her.

"Your angel is very precious to you, and it has a name; your angel's name is Charity. Your very nature is much like your angel. You are full of the love of God. The Lord is going to open your eyes to see your angel again. It is going to happen soon." Somewhere in the middle of this heavenly utterance Margaret burst into tears!

Then something else rather extraordinary began to happen. Gold dust began to rain down into the kitchen! Gold started to cover the kitchen table and our faces. After a few minutes, Margaret regained her composure, and I took a seat at the table with her. She shared with me her journey and how God had always ministered to her using the realm of angels as confirmation of everything that I had just spoken to her. We continued to fellowship together while enjoying tea and scones for the next hour and a half. Margaret gave me a copy of the book, *Good Morning, Holy Spirit.* Later, I took this Benny Hinn book along with me into the wilderness of Newfoundland where I had a life-changing encounter with the Holy Spirit in a tiny cabin.

Margaret and I were joined by two friends for breakfast, and the Lord continued to move. Jennifer received the revelation that she was supposed to give an angel's feather she had found to our hostess. When she did, the glory of God fell in the tiny kitchen. Suddenly, we all knew that we needed to pray. Margaret grabbed her head and declared that she was in intense pain. At that second I said, "My hands are on fire!"

She said, "Pray for my head."

I thought, *I have never prayed for anyone to be healed.* However, the moment I touched her, that same whispering voice began to speak into my left ear. I just repeated what I heard whispered into my left ear, and she was instantly healed.

Jennifer said, "I have a large tumor on my calf. Pray for me too!"

Again the same still, small voice led my prayers, and the tumor instantly vanished. Clara had a rotator cuff injury, and again as I prayed led by the still, small voice, she was also healed.

Then Margaret said, "I have..."

However, I interrupted her and yelled, "Stop! You have a cyst on the top of your right leg. It is the size of a pea, and when you try to play your guitar it stings and burns when you set your guitar on your leg. You have had this condition for about eight years!"

She was amazed, but no more than I, and said, "How do you know that?"

I said, "I don't know, but let me pray for you." The cyst immediately disappeared!

I sat down stunned. The others were talking excitedly. I was certain that the angel Jesus had assigned to me in the heavens was standing beside me as I had prayed and prophesied to the women. I could hear the angel whisper in my ear, and I just repeated what I was told. This is an example of how people can work in harmony with the Holy Spirit, angels, and the gifts of the spirit to impact their environment. I was lost in my thoughts, *Oh, Lord, what are you doing with me?* I had begun the astonishing process of learning to work with angels. Later I would point to this experience in Margaret's kitchen as the time when the Lord chose to birth a healing ministry through me. Sometimes I know that the healing angel is present to help Kathy and me as we pray for the sick. It only took about ten minutes for the Lord to astonish me again.

As I continued to exercise my spiritual senses with all of the spiritual tools discussed earlier, my ability to recognize angelic activity increased greatly. In addition, the Lord was showing me how angels work in symphony with the Holy Spirit to release His Kingdom on earth. It is crucial that we are in intimate relationship with the precious Holy Spirit. From this place of intimacy, we can be launched into our destinies. The Holy Spirit also encouraged me to begin to "entertain the angels" that are always around me—and you. The metamorphosis Jesus had initiated in my life was accelerated by what transpired next (see Heb. 13:2).

Chapter 4

WALKING WITH ANGELS IN THE COOL OF THE DAY

Ashort time later I felt someone poke me hard in the left arm. I turned to see who it was, but there was no one there. At the time, I dismissed it and returned my attention to my thoughts. After a minute I was poked again, only this time the poke was accompanied with an audible voice! The Holy Spirit said, "I want to go for a walk with you in the cool of the day." I jumped up totally flabbergasted. I quickly left the room and grabbed my coat, telling everyone that I was going for a walk in the "cool of the day." It just happened to be minus 12 degrees Fahrenheit (or minus 24 Celsius)!

The moment I walked out the door, the presence of the Holy Spirit fell upon me, and I began to weep again. The tears were starting to freeze on my cheeks, but I did not mind. God began to talk to me in an audible voice. I was walking through the streets of Botwood in the presence of the Holy Ghost. I could also sense that many angels were accompanying us. The angels were laughing and singing as we strolled along the snow-covered streets. It was about 8:00 A.M.

The Holy Spirit led me along a road which was on the shore of the North Atlantic Ocean. For the first time since leaving the house, I began to notice that it was very cold. However, it was worth it to be in the presence of the Lord. I was directed to a small breezeway that leads out over the Bay of Exploits (this name truly proved to be quite prophetic) to a tiny island called Killick Island. As we were walking across the breezeway, the wind was whipping off the ocean at about 40 knots. Combined with the negative temperature, the wind was turning my skin numb, and my tears had crystallized into ice on my face and mustache.

THE CITY OF REFUGE

I said, "Holy Spirit, it is really cold out here, and my face is turning numb." The Lord replied, "Do not fear; when we get onto this island, there will be a city of refuge." I had no idea what a city of refuge was, but I hoped that it would be warm and safe. (See Numbers 35:25.) The winter's day had turned even colder and grayer; there was no sun, and the dark gray sky was totally overcast. Snow was falling lightly, and being blown about by a brisk wind.

As we walked onto Killick Island, it got even colder and windier. The Holy Spirit whispered to me, "Do not fear; the city of refuge is just up these steps, hidden in those fir trees." When I ascended a few dozen steps, I saw a small stand of fir trees to the left. Just before I stepped into the middle of them, a shaft of brilliant bright light, a lone sunbeam, cracked the sky to illuminate the city of refuge. When I entered the little circle of fir trees, what the Holy Spirit had called a "city of refuge," I encountered the manifest glory of God. Angels were everywhere. It was 8:50 A.M. As we entered, I walked through some kind of invisible barrier. Surprisingly, inside the city of refuge, the temperature was very pleasant, even warm. The bright beam of sunlight slashed into the cold, gray atmosphere. As this heavenly light hit the fresh snow, there appeared to be rainbows of colors that seemed to radiate from the trees, tickling my eyes.

Suddenly, the Holy Spirit began to ask me questions. The Lord asked me to "describe what you are seeing." Every color of the rainbow seemed to dance from the tiny snowflakes as they slowly drifted and floated down from Heaven to earth. A myriad of colors reflected through the little haven.

There was a kaleidoscope of chromatic activity peppering my retinas. The heavenly array was stunning and quite spectacular to behold. I stood transfixed and mesmerized as the sunbeams danced off each one of God's miniature creations. Each snowflake seemed to emit a new colorimetric quality as it twisted and fell slowly to earth. I was seeing florescent hues that I had never encountered before. Vivid colors fluoresced throughout our secret city of refuge. I seemed to be hidden with God for a mystical moment of time. My mind began to whirl as I tried to formulate an answer to His request to "describe what I was seeing."

I began to tell the Lord how beautiful His creation was. Of course He was already aware of that, so I described how marvelous were the works of His hands and how utterly fantastic it was that each tiny snowflake was different. I described how wonderful the colors of the rainbow were and how they represented His covenant with man. The Lord was patient and allowed me to carry on in this fashion for several minutes, but alas, I was not really able to accurately answer His simple request. Then He spoke to me and gave me the revelation to what I was seeing.

The Lord said, "My son, what you are seeing are the souls of unsaved men and women of earth who are dying and going to hell at this very moment." Those words penetrated my spirit like a sharp two-edged sword. I fell to my knees and began to weep as a passion that I had never known began to well up from some mysterious and hidden place deep within my spirit. "Oh, God, look at all of those souls," I said, breaking the silence.

Suddenly, I was overwhelmed with a strange compulsion to watch for a long time as thousands upon thousands of tiny flakes fell through the bright sunbeam. Their short fall was full of spectacular color and glory, but when they hit the ground, it was all over. The Lord was revealing to me a prophetic picture of the brevity of our short lives on an eternal scale. Our days on earth are but a vapor! (See Psalm 39:5 and James 4:14.) I was pierced through to the very heart.

"Lord!" I cried out. "What can I possibly do?"

He replied, "Just do what I ask, and preach the Cross of Christ."

"I can do that Lord. I will do that, my God, but I will need Your help."

I stayed upon my knees for a long time gazing at this spectacle. During this encounter, God birthed within me a holy passion and hunger to witness souls saved and people totally healed and delivered. I was absorbed in witnessing the array of tiny cascades of colors that luxuriated in the glory of God. I contemplated the ramifications of what I had been told.

What a beautiful and glorious God He is. How can we as humankind turn our backs upon Him and such a great salvation that is so easily ours? I pondered all of the events that had been unfolding over the past few days, realizing that I would never be the same. I also realized that God would have to bring all the things that He had birthed in my heart to pass. I purposed to surrender my life and destiny to His will, and to Him. I "altared" my destiny into the hands of God.

It was also during this encounter that the Lord instructed me to travel to Africa as an "armor bearer," to preach His Gospel there and to pray for the sick. I was actually terrified by the prospect of traveling to Africa. I couldn't imagine that in reality I could go there, considering my current financial situation and my lack of training to preach or minister in healing. However, I soon learned that with God nothing is impossible. Perhaps my obedience to walk with God in minus 12 degree temperatures opened the door to Africa to me? It was still another seemingly bizarre and peculiar gesture of obedience to the Spirit of God.

ENTERTAINING ANGELS IN AMERICA

After my return to the United States from Canada, I was radically transformed. I could no longer settle for a form of godliness. I began to wait on God, and He began to release supernatural provision into my life to share the Gospel. I would lock myself in the house and lay upon my bed pondering the night in Botwood when I was transported in the spirit and taken by the angel into the very presence of Jesus for six hours. I would ask the Holy Spirit to bring to my remembrance all the things that Jesus both taught and revealed to me about my future in Him. The Lord had called me to the nations to preach His Word and to save the lost, but I could not imagine how these things could possibly come to pass.

At times, after I had been in the house for 48, 72, or 96 hours fasting and praying, the atmosphere of Heaven would invade 121 Beech Street. The tiny house would become infused with the glory and presence of God. Angelic activity would explode. The fragrance of the Lord would manifest in a powerful way. I could sense the angels as they arrived. I could hear them, and at times I could see them sitting on my couch. Often, people would walk into the house and get immediately "drunk in the spirit." They would sit on the couch and ask me what I had been doing in the house. "Just praying," I would say, never bothering to tell them that an angel was sitting beside them!

I would entertain the angels when they arrived, and welcome them. At times, they would begin to get a little "rowdy," and I could hear them and perceive them with greater clarity. It became exciting to go home and enter into the presence of the Kingdom of God, which was made manifest in the little house.

THE POWER OF GOD FELL

As I was pressing into the Kingdom with prayer and fasting, something amazing began to happen. From the moment that I would arrive home, unlock the door, and step into the house, the power of God would fall. Several times I simply fell prostrate upon the floor near the front door. I would lay in the weighty presence of God's manifest glory for hours. During these times, the Holy Spirit would hover around my body, and I would just luxuriate in His presence. At other times, I would enter my little prayer closet, and the presence of God would "bond" me to the floor. At these times, I would often be "taken out" into the heavens.

Often during such times of prayer, I would enter into the spirit, and I would be invited to come into the presence of Jesus. The Lord would take me into places in the heavenly realms, always accompanied by angels. We would visit the still waters of Psalm 23, or I would find Jesus in the Great Banquet Hall. There we would usually dine together. We also visited the stables, vineyard, library, and many of the vaults in Heaven. After most of these encounters, I would return to home with divine revelation and would have a sovereign knowledge of some detail of the Scriptures, or direction for life or ministry. (I will illustrate many of these heavenly experiences in the third book of this trilogy: *Dancing With Angels 3: Angels in the Realms of Heaven.* So look for that book in the near future if you are interested in seeing what your home in Heaven will look like, and the other places found in the heavenly realms!)

One noticeable dividend from these heavenly encounters was the fact that a greatly increased amount of grace and favor was manifested in my life. The other bonus was the fact that I was growing more comfortable with angels and their presence in my everyday life. I want to share one such encounter that relates specifically to our quest.

On the evening of March 25, 2002, I experienced a powerful encounter with the angelic realm. It was almost exactly 120 days to the minute from the night when I had the encounter with Jesus in Springdale on November 25, 2001. I was lying on the floor in the presence of the Lord when Colossians 3:1-3 manifested in my life: *"If then you were raised with Christ, seek those things which are above, where Christ is, sitting at the right hand of God. Set your mind on things above, not on things on the earth. For you died, and your life is hidden with Christ in God."*

A weighty glory began to fill the little room; I saw a brief image of Jesus in my mind's eye. "Lord, do You want me to come to You?" I asked.

He nodded yes.

I acquiesced. Immediately, I was "sucked" out of my body and was taken up in the spirit.

When I came into the presence of Jesus, He was smiling and happy to see me again, but no more than I. The Lord began to show me the ways that He would confirm and release me to activate the angel of provision He had assigned to me earlier. Somehow I understood that the time was fast approaching for me to begin to employ this angel in a greater degree. When this encounter was over, I returned to my tiny prayer room with a sovereign knowledge that some things were about to drastically change in my life. I had an understanding that the angel of provision would become very important to these upcoming events. In hindsight, I understand that the Lord was preparing me to take the next step of our journey and move me toward my personal metamorphosis. He was preparing me to go to the next level pertaining to angelic ministry and understanding how to work with God's angels.

The Lord is in the midst of releasing many angels of provision into the realm of earth at this hour. I believe that many people will be assigned angels of provision. These angels will work with you to release finances that will allow you to complete the things that are on your heart. For some it will be evangelism. For others it will be ministering to widows and orphans. Whatever God has placed upon your heart, He can empower angelic ministry to release the provision to accomplish the task.

You can access this area of angelic ministry. You do not need to be a superstar or person of great faith. These angels are going to be released to ordinary people. Let's shift our focus to Africa, and look at how Jesus is actually releasing angels to impact the earth on the African continent.

Chapter 5

ANGELS AND THE
LAMB OF GOD

After returning to America and learning to entertain angels, the Lord gave me grace, favor, and provision to travel to Tanzania. This happened when Jesus instructed me to release the angel of provision which He had assigned to me. Within eight hours, my business supernaturally prospered. The monies needed for the trip to Africa were in my bank account within 48 hours. For the sake of our topic, I will skip the myriad of other miracles that transpired in order to get us into Africa in 2002. On Tuesday, May 28, 2002, I was in Mwanza, Tanzania, in bungalow 4 at the Hotel Tilapia. The Lord had begun to stir my spirit, and I was not able to sleep very much on that trip. Time after time, the Holy Spirit would awaken me and lead me in prayer.

On that particular night, the Lord called me to prayer at 2 A.M. The Holy Spirit began to lead me to pray through the

Psalms. I was praying the Word of God while anointing the bungalow with oil that my friend and mentor Omega Dowell had given me for the trip. Suddenly I began to pray in the Spirit. It seemed that I was not praying, but God was praying through me. I had never experienced such a powerful time of intercession.

It was an amazing night. It seemed that I was a spectator. I was hearing myself pray, but was somehow detached from the intercession as an individual. This was the first time that I received understanding of what the apostle Paul meant when he wrote about Spirit-led intercession in Romans 8:26-28.

WAVES OF HIS GLORY

The spirit of prayer came upon me for about two hours. It was about 4:15 A.M. when I felt a release to cease walking around the room praying in the Spirit. I positioned a chair in the center of the room and knelt in front of it. My elbows were on the seat, and my knees were on the cold tile floor. Suddenly I began to feel waves of glory wash through the room. It was as if I was at the beach and small wavelets were hitting my knees. At first they were only about 1 or 2 inches tall. As time passed, they became larger and more pronounced. Finally the waves of glory were up to my waist, and the presence of Jesus began to invade the room.

Soon, a large wave hit me in the spirit, and I was actually knocked from the kneeling position onto the floor. However, when I fell to the floor, it was no longer a tile floor in a bungalow in Africa. I fell upon my side and landed upon a beautiful, warm, exotic, and cozy beach. I could smell the purity of the water and began to feel the gentle tides as they rolled in and washed around my prostrate body. Once again, I found that I was not able to move. I was glued to this heavenly beach much as I had been those nights in Newfoundland, and later in my little prayer closet. The waves and water began to wash around my body, cleaning and refreshing me. These waves of glory actually moved me around on the floor in the natural like a tide would do on a beach on earth. When I opened my eyes, I was able to see the crystal clear waters that stretched out in front of me (see Ps. 42:7).

I was lying on my left side facing the sea. I began to hear angelic worship with the ethereal sounds of harps, violins, and singing. I was luxuriating in the presence of the Lord. The waters were clean and pure and seemed to go on forever. In the distance, the clear water appeared very still and looked almost like a mirror. I just relaxed in this wonderful place over a long period of time. Beyond the horizon, I could see the bright sun rising out of the water. It was glorious to behold. As it rose, the sky became my focus of attention. Every color of the rainbow seemed to illuminate the sky. The colors moved and fluoresced, and the sea of glass-like crystal reflected these wonderful visual delicacies. I was reminded of how the snow-flakes emitted the colorimetric display on the Bay of Exploits in the city of refuge.

As the waves of glory washed around my body, I was slowly being moved around by the billows upon the floor, yet I was on a supernatural beach. I studied the interplays of the colorful sky and the crystal sea; they were in concert with one another. I have never beheld such beauty on earth. There are really no words that can describe the glorious scene that stretched out before me. I laid there transfixed on the view for what seemed hours, basking and luxuriating in the peace and glory that surrounded me. It seemed that the colors were actually alive.

Suddenly, the brilliant light of the sun was interrupted by a silhouette. Immediately the glory multiplied, and my eyes began to water from the radiance of the light that was emitted from behind the shadow. I tried to keep my eyes focused upon the silhouette. It kept moving in my direction. In an instant, my mind understood what was occurring. The shadow was much closer now, and I was able to discern its shape. It was the Lord Christ Jesus, and He was walking across the sea of glass-like crystal. God was trekking in my direction. In the background, I could hear a symphony of angelic worship and could sense the bustle of angelic activity. I could hear a symphony of different instruments, but I could only behold the Lamb of God. (See Revelation 4:6; 15:2.)

The glory and love of God increased as the waves of crystal water continued to wash around my body. I was immobilized, but could see and hear clearly. The fragrance of the Lord became stronger as He approached. It seemed as if the sounds of the beautiful worship filled the atmosphere around the Lamb of God. The winds began to blow around me for the first time since I had "landed" upon the beach. I was now fully aware that a multitude of angels were accompanying Jesus.

THE DISCERNING OF SPIRITS

Jesus walked purposefully across the last few feet of the crystal clear water and stepped upon the beach. As He did so, His silhouette overshadowed me. Christ Jesus then stood over my body in the same way that He had in Springdale on November 25, 2001. I could feel the same glory and supernatural love that He carried for me. The sun was perfectly positioned and encircled His head. Every possible conceivable color fluoresced within the sky behind His head. I gazed into the beautiful eyes of Jesus, and He smiled at me. I was lost in the utter beauty, majesty, and grandeur of the Lord for an eternal moment. I did not want to move from that place.

The Lord began to speak to me softly as a father might speak to a small child. He told me that He was going to share some important things with me to help me when I was in Africa. I was over 15,000 miles from the place I had always called home. The Lord had returned to keep His promise to me. He had called me to the nations, and I was actually in Africa teaching, preaching, and ministering. Of course, this was made possible by the angel that Jesus had assigned to me to help release financial provision for the mission trip.

As I continued to lie upon the beach, the Lord Jesus continued to speak to me. He told me about the importance of the gift of discerning of spirits, and why discerning was crucial to ministering healing to His precious African children when ministering in the gifts of miracles and healings. The Lord had been speaking gently to me for a long time when suddenly He looked up. I was disappointed that Jesus took His gaze from me and stopped His steady flow of words and instruction. The Lord was sensing my discomfort and smiled at me, and then looked off to His right again.

I knew that He would continue His teaching shortly, so I relaxed and watched to see what would happen next.

A PROCESSION OF ANGELS

Then I saw a powerful angel walk up to Jesus. The Lord spoke to this angel, although I did not understand the words that passed back and forth between them. However, I did understand that this angel had been working in Tanzania and had been on an important assignment. I really do not understand how I knew what was transpiring. I just had a supernatural revelation of what was taking place as the Lord stood over me and gave instruction to the angel. Perhaps just being so close to the Lord allowed me to have some understanding of the things that were unfolding before me in the spirit.

Shortly, I saw this angel "ascend" upon Jesus. I knew that this angel was returning into the realms of Heaven, and that the assignment that it had been on had now been completed. I was astonished to see the angel ascend into the heavens "on" Jesus. It was very similar to the night in Springdale when I saw Jesus ascend back through the open heaven spinning in the sanctuary in Living Waters Church. (See John 1:51.) The Lord looked at me and gave me a big smile. He began to speak to me again, just as a loving friend would to a small child. In just a moment or two, He was again interrupted by a second strong angel.

This time the angel descended from the realms of Heaven upon Jesus and stepped onto the beach. Once again the Lord and the angel began to speak, though again I was unable to understand the language that they spoke. I could see this second angel was powerful and very strong. He carried himself in the manner of a warrior, and there was a large sword in his right hand. He also had a large, polished, shiny golden shield in his left hand. Upon his belt were other weapons, including an ornate buckler and a smaller type of sword. As I was looking, I suddenly saw Jesus pat the angel upon his powerful shoulder and point with His right hand. Immediately, the angel turned in military fashion and ran off in the direction that the Lord had indicated. I was astonished, but I was also absolutely certain that Jesus had just commissioned the strong second angel to an important mission in the nation of Tanzania.

Then Jesus turned His loving gaze back upon me as I lay on the beach. The waters were still billowing around me. The Lord again began to speak to me and told me that it was important that I began to study and learn to understand about the "seer anointing." At that moment, I did not have any knowledge of the seer anointing, so I was a little concerned about my ignorance. As if sensing I was uncomfortable, the Lord smiled and gently began to speak with me about the seer prophets of old.

This encounter with the Lord continued from about 4:15 A.M. until about 6:30 A.M. in the natural. However, in the realm of the spirit, it seemed to last for many more hours. The Lord continued to speak to me in great detail about the seer gift or anointing. I could determine the passage of time because the sun shifted its position over the sea of glass-like crystal as He continued to speak. The other reason I was aware of time passing was that there began to be a steady stream of angels ascending and descending upon the Lord Jesus Christ.

ANGELS ON MISSIONS

This procession of angels was quite impressive. After the first few, I began to relax. I had been uncertain if the Lord would continue to speak to me as each angel who appeared would interrupt His words. Jesus would greet each angel, and then they would either ascend or depart out into the continent of Africa to embark on a supernatural mission. I would estimate that I witnessed over 100 angels interact with the Lord Jesus during this time. Often, the ones who seemed to come from the regions of Africa seemed to be a little fatigued, and I perceived that they had been involved in spiritual warfare in the heavenly realms over the nations of Africa. Yet each angel was in good spirits, (pun intended), and was more than glad to see the Lord Jesus. I was sure that Jesus was the commander in charge and the One who leads and deploys the angelic hosts into the temporal realm of earth.

As angels would descend upon Jesus, the Lord would speak to them and give them instructions and directions. Jesus would then take His right hand and clasp their right shoulder, smile, and release each angel. He would do this by pointing to a specific direction. Then, each descending angel would pivot with military precision and run off in the direction that the Lord had indicated. This was repeated time and time again. Between each deployment the Lord would pick up His teaching and continue to smile and speak to me. It seemed to me that the Lord was taking great pleasure in releasing these angels and placing them on assignment. I was truly mesmerized by what I was witnessing.

Every time after an angel was deployed, it seemed that a minute or two later another angel would arrive and interact with the Lord. They would speak. Jesus would congratulate the returning angel. Then the angel would ascend into the realms of Heaven. The angels varied greatly in appearance. There seemed to be some angels who carried a much greater authority than others, but all were powerful in their own right. They were of various sizes. Some were very tall and seemed to be between 12 to 15 feet, although it was difficult to truly know from my prostrate position. Other angels were of normal human size. All of the angels seemed to be wearing white robes with sashes and assorted belts depending upon the type of gear that they were carrying. They all carried weapons and various articles of warfare.

Many of the ascending angels seemed to be very glad to be invited by the Lord to return into the realms of Heaven. Many of the descending angels also seemed to be just as excited to be employed by Jesus into the assignments and realms of earth. However, the one who seemed to be the most pleased with these events was Jesus Himself. The Lord was commissioning many of these angels in answer to the prayers of the African saints. These angels were traveling into many nations. Some of the dispatched angels were assigned to minister over individuals, individual ministries, individual villages, cities, and regions. Some of the more powerful angels were being assigned to the heavenly realms over entire nations.

Some of these angels were anointed to bring healing. Others were anointed and instructed to release the manifestation and answers to prayers. Still others were assigned to do battle with the powers and principalities over certain areas

and regions. Many of the angels were assigned to help ministers in Africa win lost souls to Jesus Christ as Savior.

I did not share this experience with anyone for several
years. Jesus had instructed me to keep these things hidden
in my heart and to ponder them as time passed. The Lord
also instructed me that He would release me to share about
the seer anointing at the appropriate season. I pondered this
encounter in my heart for years. Later, the Lord instructed me
to begin to preach and teach about the seer anointing and the
restoration of the gift of discerning of spirits. These directions
came on May 29, 2007, after a powerful vision concerning
Christ's imminent release of global revivals. We will look at
this vision in great detail later.

I was given a rare privilege to witness a multitude of the
angelic host in ministry. I witnessed how the Lord indeed
employs angels in the daily operation of the Kingdom of
Heaven. I am certain that there are many places like this
throughout the earth where the heavens are open and angels
move freely from the realms of Heaven to the earth on an
ongoing and daily basis. Some people call these places a
Mahanaim, or camp of God (see Gen. 32:2). Geographic
locations like this are also called an open heaven by some
people. (We will study this dynamic of Christ's kingdom in
great detail in the second book of this trilogy.)

This glimpse into the realm where angels dwell and interact with our world radically changed my mindset. I began
to understand that angelic activity and ministry were always
present around us. Jesus is actively working with the angelic
host to impact the lives of people on earth. One of the ways
that ordinary people can work with angels is through prayer

and intercession. The Lord will begin to open our understanding so that we can effectively co-labor with His angels in this way. Next let's look at some spiritual principles that will help you understand how to work with God's angels in prayer.

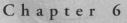

Chapter 6

WORKING WITH
ANGELS IN PRAYER

Perhaps one of the most important duties of angels is to bring the answer to people's prayers or execute God's answer to prayers in the natural realm. Answering prayer is a fundamental duty of angels. You have angels that are assigned to minister to you this way. *And of the angels He says..."Are they not all ministering spirits sent forth to minister for those who will inherit salvation?"* (Heb. 1:7,14). Angels are empowered by God to manifest the answers of the prayers of anyone—believers and non-believers, Jew or Gentile, alike. We have seen that at times the Lord can empower people to release angels to work like this by answering prayers on people's behalf.

The English word *angel* is translated from the New Testament Greek word *aggelos* which literally means "messenger or courier."[1] Many ordinary people will begin to experience this kind of angelic ministry in this season. I have been amazed as I have had opportunities to employ angels to release provision. There have been amazing and immediate answers to prayers as angels work on our behalf. I experienced many "secular miracles" or "normal miracles" immediately after Jesus assigned the angel of provision to me. All of these normal miracles helped me to establish the King of Glory Music Festival, and more importantly, my faith in God. Let's look at a few of these normal miracles. This can help you see how simple it is to work with angels in prayer.

"NORMAL MIRACLES"

One night I was working on some miniature paintings when my friend Sue Burnopp—Mrs. Sue—called me. She told me that her grandson had been in a bad car accident in Florida. Her daughter needed to get an airline ticket to fly to be at his side. Mrs. Sue asked me to join in prayer with her according to the principle of Matthew 18:19. As she told me this, the Lord whispered into my ear, "You can release _____ (the angel's name), to go and make a way for her daughter to get a ticket." As she told me about the situation, I said a little heart's prayer and did as the Lord had instructed, releasing the angel of provision to go in the name of Jesus. We began to pray and had prayed only about 30 seconds when she stopped and said, "I'm getting a beep; it may be my daughter. Let me check, and then we will finish praying."

I waited on the line for about two minutes while she took the call. While I waited, I also prayed and was actually giving the Lord glory for the airline ticket that He had "already provided." When Sue got back on the line, she was excited!

"Praise God! That was my daughter! She got the ticket! The airline just called her and gave her a ticket; she is leaving for Florida in the morning!"

To be honest, I was stunned. Later, I realized that when the Lord spoke to me telling me to release the angel of provision, incredible miracles happened. I will always remember the night my precious friend Mrs. Sue called me. It was an epiphany to me about the validity of angelic ministry and how Jesus allows people to release or "loose" angels to manifest the answer to prayer.

In June 2003, I had been led by the Lord to apply for a discipleship program with a well-known ministry. I had only one small problem. The program was an investment of $25,000, and I had $25. However, I trusted the Lord to provide the funds. During that time, I was in ministry with my friend Charlie Robinson. We were at Extreme Church in Las Vegas. Charlie preached, and I helped to pray for the sick. As I raised my hands in worship that morning on July 6, 2003, I began to feel the "winds blow" around my head, and I smelled the wonderful aroma of frankincense—I knew angels were close at hand.

My concentration on Jesus' presence was broken by His voice. Jesus said, "Kevin, I want to show you something." Without opening my eyes or losing focus, I replied, "OK, Lord, what do you wish for me to see?" Instantly I saw a football field. The football field was massive, perhaps miles in length and width. It was brilliant green and marked with the yard lines. Suddenly, the lines began to dance and move in the "eyes of my heart." The eyes of my understanding were opened or enlightened to see what Jesus had for me as an inheritance that morning. This was the "seer anointing" at work.

The lines of the football field continued a metamorphosis and were transformed into a huge $5,000 bill. In this vision, I also saw the Lord Jesus standing by and smiling at me. Christ looked like a proud father about to give a small child a new bicycle on Christmas morning. The Lord was beaming with pleasure. The same four angels I had seen before were now standing behind Christ Jesus. The angels seemed quite happy to be witnessing all this transpire.

The Lord pointed, and the lines of the bill began to dance around in the vision. In an instant, the supernatural currency was transformed again. Only this time it reassembled a $20,000 bill! I said, "Lord, I know that there is no such thing as a $5,000 bill, and I know that there is no such thing as a $20,000 bill. Lord, what am I seeing?"

The Lord said, "Kevin, those are two checks. They are the monies you need for the discipleship program. Pray for them now. Loose _____ (the angel's name) to go forth and release them from the realms of Heaven."

"OK, Lord," I said. And I began to pray a brief prayer something like, "Father, in the name of Jesus, I loose _____ to go forth and bring in these two checks. I call in the check for $5,000 to manifest and come forth; I call in the check for $20,000 to manifest and to come forth, in the name of Jesus Christ, Amen."

Jesus smiled at me again, and I saw one of the angels scamper away. Just as quickly as the vision began it was over. However I had a "knowing" that the Lord would certainly supply the monies for the discipleship program.

After returning home, I was praying when I got a phone call from a man from the West Coast. I did not know the person very well. He told me that he and his wife had been praying for me, and they believed that they were being led by the Lord to "sow into the discipleship program on my behalf." I was stunned as he told me this. He went on to say that they were going to give $5,000. Seventy-two hours later I received another phone call from the West Coast. The person told me that they had been praying and that the Lord had been speaking to them about the discipleship program. A lump formed in my throat.

The person said, "The Lord had been telling me to help you. Honestly, I have been disobedient...I was supposed to call you three days ago about this, but I wanted to be sure. How much money do you need for the discipleship program?"

My mind was racing. How on earth could I tell this person that I needed $20,000? Suddenly, the Holy Spirit whispered into my left ear, "Just tell them what you need."

I took a deep breath and said, "I still need twenty thousand."

A short silence hung in the air, and then they said, "That is the exact amount that I heard from the Lord. Where do you want me to send the monies?"

I was speechless.

"Hello? Are you still there?"

We talked for a few more minutes, but I am not sure what I said. I was in a state of shock. The Lord had done it. The two checks that Jesus had shown me in the vision were actually given to me within 96 hours of Sunday, July 6, 2003. The angel of provision had worked quickly and efficiently.

God has instructed and allowed me to release this angel of provision on more than one occasion. I was accepted for the discipleship program on July 7. This is an area of angelic ministry that is available to anyone at this hour. The key to this kind of angelic ministry is to have intimacy and friendship with Jesus.

ANGEL OF PROVISION HELPS AGAIN

I have already shared about the way this angel of provision had provided funds for my first mission trip. That angel also saved the trip for me in another way. Prior to my first mission trip to Africa, I was required to acquire a visa stamp by sending my U.S. passport to the Tanzanian Embassy in Washington, DC, to get the stamp. Unfortunately, my passport had gone missing in the U.S. mail for several weeks. Unless I received my passport within a few days, I would not be allowed to travel internationally.

I was due to fly from Roanoke, Virginia, on Tuesday. It was Friday, and I still did not have a passport. I began to fast and pray. I was becoming increasingly concerned that I would miss the trip and forfeit all the blessings and finances that were associated with it. I prayed all day Friday, and there was no breakthrough. I continued to pray all morning Saturday. Later that afternoon, the mailman stepped onto the porch. I heard his heavy footsteps as he walked across the wooden porch. Then I heard the unmistakable sound of the old, rusty, black metal mailbox being opened, "eeeeerrrrkkkk, thud!"

I thought, *At last the passport is here!* I sprang up from my prayer room and quickly moved to the front door to collect my passport. When I opened the mailbox, there was only a bill and no passport. I was now at the point of believing that I would not be able to travel to Africa. Since I was scheduled to leave Tuesday, that meant there was just one more mail delivery day. Rather than give up, I purposed in my heart to press into prayer and fasting all the more. So with this renewed vigor, I began to cry out to the Lord.

In the middle of my prayer—and whining—I saw something. I had a quick short vision of the time when the Lord spoke to me and told me that He was releasing an angel to help me by giving me provision and protection. I saw Jesus with the four angels. In that brief moment of silence, I clearly heard the Lord say, "Kevin, just loose _____ (the angel's name) to go forth, find your passport, and bring it to you."

I prayed a simple prayer: "Father, I ask You now in the name of Jesus Christ; I need that passport, and I loose _____ (the angel's name) to go forth and bring my passport to me. _____, go and find the passport and bring it to me here now. In Jesus' name I pray, amen."

It was about 2:30 A.M., and I was exhausted and frustrated. I decided to read the Word. So I took my Bible and began to read the Gospels. I fell into a deep sleep about 3:30 A.M. on Sunday morning with my trusty King James Bible open across my chest. It was not long before I was startled to consciousness by a familiar sound, "eeeeerrrrkkkk, thud!" I was immediately wide awake. I thought, *That was the sound of the mailbox!* But it was 5:30 on Sunday morning, and the USPS definitely does not deliver mail on Sundays!

The sound and these thoughts all transpired in less than three seconds. I leaped off of my bed and ran to the front door, ripping it open. The sky was just beginning to turn to a gentle shade of light blue, and the morning was just beginning to dawn. There was no mailman on the porch. I ran to the sidewalk in my bare feet and quickly glanced up and down Beech Street. Nothing. There was not a soul in sight. It had been less than ten seconds since I had heard the sound!

I could feel the glory of God resting on my front porch and washing through the street. Slowly I made my way to the old black mailbox. "Eeeeeeeeerrrrkkkk," I slowly lifted the top with my right hand. It was still too dark to see. I carefully reached into the old mailbox with my left hand. There was something there. I slowly pulled out my hand and was astonished to see my lost passport in it.

There is no explanation other than angelic intervention and ministry. Surely no human hand had placed that missing passport in the mailbox; rather, it was the hand of God moving through angelic ministry. The passport was not in any carton, container, or any type of mailing envelope. It just appeared in the mailbox! The trip to Tanzania was imperative for me as Jesus met me there in a powerful way.

Angels also minister to people by giving or manifesting provision. Many times this takes the form of finding lost articles, like a passport, as in my case, or a set of keys. The enemy will often seek to hide something that is needed and important. Angels are ready, willing, and able to help recover these things. Here is another classic testimony of this kind.

Kathy and I have a friend in Exeter, England. Andrew Pearkes is perhaps the most humble man I have ever known. Andrew has also experienced numerous angelic encounters. He is often able to see or perceive what angels are doing in our midst. Andrew has been touched by angels and healed many times.

> I have had numerous occasions where angels have come to bring messages to me, to comfort me, and strengthen me in some of the very long meetings I have done...the longest 12.5 hours. They [angels] lift up my arms, and many see them. I have experienced many miracles performed by angels. Many times I have been protected by angels from assaults in meetings. Many other times, I have experienced angelic ministry in the areas of protection, healing, miracles, and much more.
>
> —Andrew Pearkes
> Maranatha Ministries, Exeter, England

On one such occasion, Andrew had to travel from Exeter to Dudley, about a three-and-a-half hour drive, to attend a conference. Andrew decided to leave the first thing in the morning at about 7 as he had to get there by 10:30 a.m. As he was about to leave, he picked up the car keys from the dining room table and drove off in his car toward Bristol. When he was near Bristol, he noticed that he was low on fuel, so he pulled off the highway into a service station.

As he was at the fuel pump starting to remove the cap, he discovered that there was no key to open the fuel tank on the key ring! I remember Andrew's words as he related this story to me; he said, "I was in a big pickle," and he gave a big belly laugh. He went to ask the owner if they had any spare keys to fit the lock on his cap. The man gave Andrew a cardboard box which contained about 50 fuel cap keys. Andrew returned to the car and tried the various keys, but none opened the lock. Feeling defeated, Andrew stood up straight and placed his elbows on the roof of the car. He called out to the Lord. "Father, Your Word says that You are my ever-present help in times of trouble. Lord, I am in trouble, and I need help... *Help*," he declared, quoting Psalm 46:1.

Andrew said that immediately after he had prayed, he turned to see a man emerge from behind a white metal building about 200 feet (60 meters) away. As this man dressed in normal clothes approached Andrew, he noticed that the man had a key in his right hand! Andrew said, "He had the most amazing and beautiful smile as he approached me, full of peace and love. The man came to the car and opened the cap with his key. Then he looked up and smiled at me. He didn't talk, even though I asked him his name, and then he turned and walked away around the back of the same building. The amazing thing was that in his hand he had the right key!"

Andrew knew this man was an angel, and he thanked the Lord who was truly His ever-present help in time of trouble. When Andrew arrived at the conference he was very late, so he went in quietly in back of those who were worshiping. Andrew had a very serious injury to his left shoulder. Nearly two years before, he had an accident and tore three ligaments out of the bones; his arm was useless and caused him great pain. He had waited 17 months for an operation as the Lord had not healed him. After the operation, he had five months of physiotherapy and was left with 30 percent usage in the arm and more than 75 percent wasting in the muscles.

While Andrew was worshiping at the back of the meeting, someone came up from behind and smacked Andrew's left shoulder three times so hard that he felt it and heard it! He looked around, and there was no one there! He said he knew that he was healed, and he immediately lifted his arm—as he did, all the muscles grew back, and his arm became strong! An angel had touched Andrew and healed him. Andrew was checked by the surgeon who said, "This is totally impossible. You have 100 percent usage and rotation in your shoulder; your muscles are restored. This is a miracle."

MOM'S BURNING BUSH

I moved from 121 Beech Street in late 2003. I had been unwilling to leave the little house even after the Lord had begun to show me that He was positioning me for something new. The Lord had instructed me to move back to 1212 East Drive and to stay with my mother for a season. I did not understand the move at that time. Looking back on it now, I can see that the Lord had me stay with Mom to help her understand some things from His Word and His Kingdom. Many times we would discuss the Scriptures and the supernatural.

Mom was starting to embrace the supernatural as I had given her some literature on the subject. She was enthralled with the passages about miracles and the ministry of angels. We talked about these things a number of times. As a result, Mom shared several supernatural encounters that she had experienced as a young woman. We looked at the Scriptures together to find confirmation for her in God's Word. She seemed to take great comfort in this.

After I had been living at Mom's for about six months, I understood that God had placed me there to share His heart with her. She had harbored a lot of bitterness and unforgiveness. During that time, I was able to show her in the Word of God that it was vital that she should forgive and release people that she may have held anger, grudges, or bitterness against. We talked about these things for about three months. Finally she told me that she did not think that she could forgive some of the people who had wronged her or her children. I told her to pray about it.

One morning I awoke to find Mom crying at the kitchen table. I could tell that she had encountered the Lord. She had her Bible open and was searching the Word just as we had been doing together to interpret supernatural experiences. I asked her if she wanted to talk to me, but she said no. I knew that this was something that she would have to work out on her own. A few days later, she finally asked me to talk to her.

She said, "Kevin, I think that I may be losing my mind. I had been praying and was really asking God about what you had told me about forgiveness. I told the Lord that I was not able to forgive certain people, and that He was going to have to give me a sign. Well, about an hour later, I had a strong desire to get up and go into the kitchen. When I did, I heard the Lord speaking to me. He said, 'Helen, Helen, come here.' When I looked out the kitchen window, I saw the azalea bush burning. I looked at it for the longest time, and I could have sworn that the Lord was speaking to me out of that bush! Kevin, it was really burning with a beautiful blue flame. I could not take my eyes off of it.

"I watched the bush burn for the longest time, and it was like God was just speaking directly into my heart. I could feel His love. I have never felt anything like that before. God told me that what His Word said was true. He told me what I needed to do. I cried like I have never cried before in my whole life. I prayed and forgave everyone, and a really strong peace came to me. The whole time I was watching the azalea bush burn. But now I think that maybe I am losing my mind. What do you think?"

"Mom, that is awesome! Let's get the Bible out and see what it says," I said.

I instinctively turned to Exodus 3 and told Mom to read about Moses and the burning bush. She said, "That is exactly what happened to me! I have been looking in the New Testament. I never thought to look in the Old Testament." Mom's countenance took on a new luster.

"Do you really think that God would speak to me like that from a burning bush?"

I laughed. "Sure, Mom, He loves you very much."

Mom was about 80 years of age when this happened, and from that day forward, I saw a new tenderness and gentleness in her. I believe that the Lord spoke to my mother just as He did Moses and prepared her heart to enter into her heavenly home. After that day, from time to time, I would find Mom at the kitchen window looking out at the azalea bush praying to the Lord. She was a new creation after that encounter.

Mom's testimony is a great example of how the Lord can use angels to answer prayers and to give ordinary people important messages from the realms of Heaven. Was there an angel in the azalea bush? I feel certain that there was. Just before my mother passed away, I was with her in the hospital, and she also saw angels in her room. The Lord had activated the gift of discerning of spirits in Mom's life giving her hope, peace, and comfort.

Another common activity that angels are involved in is worship. I'll share several incredible testimonies about angels who have manifested during times of worship in the next chapter. These testimonies can help massage your faith and prepare you to recognize angelic activity in worship settings.

ENDNOTE

1. "Aggelos"; see http://www.studylight.org/lex/grk/view.cgi ?number=3.

Chapter 7

ANGELS AND PRAISE AND WORSHIP

One of the key ministries of angels is to worship God. We have entered into a time when the Lord will begin to activate and "open the eyes and ears" of ordinary people to experience angelic worship. Throughout the canon of Scripture, angels are described as singing (see Rev. 4:8). They also carry and play musical instruments at times (see Rev. 8:2-6; 1 Thess. 4:16). I have already shared my testimony of how the angels joined in with the worship teams in Canada. In those meetings, many individuals heard angelic voices and instruments during the worship.

Angels are fond of singing worship songs to the Lord and seem to get very excited during times of worship. This is a very common manifestation of angelic ministry today. Many saints testify to hearing angelic singing in worship services at various times and locations. One of the most opportune times to massage your ability to perceive angels is in times of worship. (See Revelation 7:11 and Psalm 103:20.)

At times, angels play instruments; I have witnessed them singing and playing small instruments on a few occasions. I have never seen on earth an instrument built like the ones the angels play. I have seen many different kinds of instruments angels make use of. Angels play woodwind and stringed instruments, horn and trumpet types of instruments, and even percussion instruments. I can only say they looked like lyres, harps, xylophones, and many other kinds of ancient stringed instruments. Angels are extremely skilled at music and worship. There are many references to musical instruments that may possibly be associated with angelic worship found in the Psalms alone. (See Psalm 6:1; 33:2; 57:8; 81:2; 92:3; 98:5; 108:2; 149:3; 150:3.)

ANGELIC WORSHIP

I love the words of angels that are immortalized in Scripture. Luke 2:8-14 is amazing! The Bible actually records the words of angelic worship songs:

> *Now there were in the same country shepherds living out in the fields, keeping watch over their flock by night. And behold, an angel of the Lord stood before them, and the glory of the Lord shone around them, and they were greatly afraid* (Luke 2:8-9).

Notice the shepherd's fearful response to the angelic visitors and the first words the heavenly visitor speaks to them!

Then the angel said to them, "Do not be afraid,
for behold, I bring you good tidings of great joy
which will be to all people. For there is born to
you this day in the city of David a Savior, who
is Christ the Lord."...And suddenly there was
with the angel a multitude of the heavenly host
praising God and saying [or singing]: "Glory to
God in the highest, and on earth peace, good-
will toward men!" (Luke 2:10-14)

Angels love to worship Jesus! (See also Revelation 4:8.)

A circuit-riding preacher named Robert Sheffey held large camp meetings in the mountains of Virginia in the mid-to-late 1800s. One characteristic of his popular meetings was the sounds of angelic choirs, which were occasionally said to be heard singing in unison with the worshipers. Incidentally, it is reported that Reverend Sheffey never prayed an unanswered prayer. Did Robert Sheffey have revelations of the hidden treasure of the Kingdom of God concerning angelic ministry?

In 2004, while Kathy and I were traveling in Peru, we experienced a spectacular manifestation of angelic ministry associated with worship. We were helping with a healing crusade in a large soccer stadium. There were thousands of people in attendance. At one point during the worship, almost every person on the ministry team began to hear what sounded like trumpets, horns, stringed instruments, and a choir of voices worshiping in unison with the worship team.

The heavenly worship team became so loud at one point that we began to look around the stadium to see if perhaps there was some kind of festival or band at the rear of the stadium. This heavenly music continued uninterrupted for about 45 minutes. Even when the worship team on the platform stopped playing between songs, the heavenly worship team would continue to sing and play. The music was truly ethereal.

Finally my curiosity got the better of me, so I decided to investigate the source of the music. The stadium had thick concrete walls, and the upper sections were open to the outside. It seemed and sounded to me that the heavenly music was coming in from the roof, or immediately behind the stadium. I walked up to the upper level of the stadium and then walked around the perimeter of the building. This took me about ten minutes. During this whole time, I was looking with my eyes for the source of the worship music. From my point of observation I could clearly see and hear the worship team on the platform, but it was obvious to me that the heavenly music was emanating from *above* the stadium.

The heavenly worship became very loud and pronounced, so I walked to the rear of stadium and climbed the steps to the second floor and looked down to the street below. The street was totally empty except for a few food vendors. I had been walking around for about fifteen minutes at that point. Suddenly the worship team on the platform stopped, and the minister was introduced to speak. The only problem was that someone forgot to tell the heavenly worship team, or "band of angels," to stop playing!

The minister asked the entire stadium full of people to be quiet. I had a great vantage point on the second level at the rear of the stadium. Suddenly 4,000 or so people stood still, and to the amazement of everyone, the volume of the heavenly worship began to increase dramatically. As the heavenly worship intensified, I saw what I can only describe as a purple whirlwind begin to blow and descend into the upper part of the stadium. As the volume of the angelic worship increased again, I began to see feathers float and fall from this large, whirling, "heavenly funnel cloud." The feathers began to rain down on the entire stadium, and at the same time, winds began to blow through the stadium. The wind was strong and actually began to move papers and other debris around the floor and seating area. People's clothing fluttered, and some of the people held on to their hats. Along with the wind, the power and anointing of the Holy Spirit greatly increased.

From my vantage point, I could both see and feel the environment outside. There was absolutely no wind blowing outside the stadium. The supernatural wind only blew inside the stadium. The minister asked the congregation to raise their hands if they could hear the heavenly choir. An estimated 50 percent of hands in the stadium went up. This was an unusual manifestation of angelic ministry as thousands heard angels singing and worshiping the Lord with instruments. This was also a night when hundreds prayed to receive Christ as Savior. It was one of the most powerful angelic encounters I have been part of due to the magnitude and number of people who perceived the angelic activity in our midst.

One of the most common manifestations of angelic ministry occurs in worship. This kind of angelic ministry is clearly illustrated in Scripture, and is also one of the most widely accepted types of angelic encounters today. Many know someone who has heard angels who have accompanied worship at one time or another. We will also see another amazing example of interacting with angelic worship in the next chapter. Worship events are excellent places to exercise your spiritual senses when seeking to perceive angels.

I believe that this kind of angelic ministry will continue to multiply in the coming season. As the approaching global healing revivals begin to manifest, we will begin to see more angelic collaboration in our worship. Another aspect of this kind of angelic ministry will be the release of spectacular miracles and healings as angels minister during our worship events. Their ministry will dramatically increase with those events that are orchestrated in public forums like the football and soccer stadiums around the earth. It will also manifest in small settings like "cell groups" or home group meetings, and even in the streets. We will look at this dynamic of angelic ministry in more detail later in the book.

Chapter 8

ANGELS BRING REVELATION, GUIDANCE, AND DIRECTION

We will begin to see angels give ordinary people revelation, guidance, and direction. God will begin to supernaturally position people to share the Gospel to unreached groups of people. Angelic ministry will also be utilized by the Lord to give people direction that will place them in geographic areas of safety. Some people will be anointed and empowered to reach people in the most forsaken places on earth. There are many examples of this kind of angelic ministry found in Scripture.

Philip received angelic guidance and empowerment when he encountered an angel that spoke with him in Acts 8:26-27: *"Now an angel of the Lord spoke to Philip, saying, 'Arise and go toward the south along the road which goes down from Jerusalem to Gaza.'...So he arose and went...."* Because of this encounter, the Gospel preceded the first missionaries to Ethiopia. This was a direct result of obedience to angelic guidance in Philip's life and ministry. The apostle Paul also had an angel visit him and give him direction and guidance in Acts 27:23-24. And of course Daniel also was given revelation when he was visited by Gabriel in Daniel 9:21-22. There are dozens of other examples of this kind of angelic ministry found throughout the Bible.

This aspect of angelic ministry will greatly increase with ordinary people in the coming days. Kathy and I have had a few powerful angelic encounters like these biblical examples. These visitations have shaped the course of our lives. These types of angelic visitations should not be feared but rather welcomed and embraced. However, it is important that we evaluate these types of angelic encounters thoroughly and accurately. We need wisdom in such instances. We will discuss principles to help you evaluate your angelic experiences later. I want to share two testimonies that will help give you an idea of how Jesus employs angels in this manner today.

MURCHISON FALLS, UGANDA

In 2002 I was in Africa again traveling to Jinja, Uganda, to help with another crusade. Forty-two of the mission team traveled to Murchison Falls National Park for a two-day safari before the crusade. The first night we lodged at the park before heading to Jinja. I was assigned a small "African style" hut that night. I was surprised to have a single room. I was really excited about the trip and was hoping that the Lord would meet me as He did previously in Tanzania. I was not surprised when a spirit of prayer came on me at about 10 P.M. I began to intercede and pray in the Spirit. This was exactly what happened when I was visited by Jesus at the sea of glass-like crystal. (See Zechariah 12:10.)

I prayed for hours as the Holy Spirit led me. I actually prayed all night. At about 3:30 A.M., I had been praying for about five and a half hours when the atmosphere in the room began to change. It seemed that the heavens themselves were swirling overhead. I began to feel the anointing of the Lord, and soon the fragrance of frankincense filled the hut. I was sitting on the bed with a candle burning on a small table. I was praying in the Spirit as the glory of the Lord hovered in the hut. I prayed like this until about 5:30 A.M.

Suddenly, it seemed to me that a breeze was beginning to blow in a circle in my hut. I opened my eyes to check the time, and I noticed that the candle was actually flickering in the wind. I continued to pray until an audible voice startled me to a halt. "Kevin," it said.

I was silent, waiting to see who was at the door. "Kevin," sounded the voice a second time. Suddenly, I realized that I was hearing the Lord, and said, "Yes, Lord." I opened my eyes to see four large angels standing at attention, or on guard, around the perimeter of the little hut. They were all about 7 or 8 feet tall and seemed to be outfitted for war. They carried swords, shiny shields, and smaller swords in their sashes. They all looked mighty and strong.

Before I could continue examining them, the Lord called my name again, "Kevin, you must go to Kansas City. When the time is right, you will move to Kansas City, and you will worship at Christ Triumphant Church. You are to submit to the authority of the pastors there. Your ministry must go through Kansas City. Do you understand this?"

"Yes, Lord," I said.

When I opened my eyes again, I could no longer see the angels in the hut, but I could perceive their presence. The sun had begun to filter over the trees, and I was surprised to see that it was past 6:00 A.M. I received a great peace knowing that I was going to Kansas City, although I was not familiar with Christ Triumphant Church. I closed my eyes and was concentrating on what was spoken over me. For some reason I was not surprised that these instructions had come in the form of an audible voice because the presence of the Lord was so strong. I was curious as to what the Lord had meant when He said, "Your ministry must go through Kansas City."

A little less than two years later I received revelation about those audible words. God had sovereignly and supernaturally prospered me, totally transforming my life. When I had completed discipleship training, the first thing that Kathy and I did was to move to Kansas City. Just two days later, I was headed to Toronto, Canada, to help with an outreach in that city. I had to leave very early in the morning to catch my flight. On the way to MCI Airport, Kathy and I were driving on Route 71 North just as the sun began to rise over the skyline of the metro. I was driving straight through the heart of Kansas City. As the morning sun crested over the buildings of the metro's skyline, the brilliant light blinded me for a moment.

Then the Lord spoke to me very clearly, and His presence filled the car. He asked, "Where are you?" At that moment I was given a supernatural revelation and remembrance of the night I was in the hut at Murchison Falls. I was driving through Kansas City on my way to one of the first assignments of King of Glory Ministries International. Indeed the ministry was at that moment going through Kansas City! I was astonished at the goodness and faithfulness of the Lord! What God alone had accomplished in my life at that time was amazing and truly miraculous. The metamorphosis, supernatural transformation, and blessings that I had experienced in my life had been activated by angelic ministry. The next testimony of angelic ministry was the flash point for that metamorphosis.

DANCING WITH ANGELS

This angelic encounter manifested in the summer of 2003. A circle of angels appeared in Malawi, Africa, as I worshiped Jesus. It was during one of those manifestations of the angelic realm that the Lord spoke to me about my immediate future and an upcoming trip to Las Vegas, Nevada. This encounter with a host of angels altered my spiritual, emotional, and carnal mindset concerning the angelic realm. It birthed in me an absolute assurance pertaining to God's desire for His children to interact with His angels.

I was in Africa again to help minister with another crusade and had been asked to lead a team of twelve people on outreaches and humanitarian works in the city of Lilongwe. The team stayed at the Sunbird Capitol Hotel in Lilongwe from June 3 to June 8. From the very beginning of this mission trip, I found that I was not able to sleep. The spirit of prayer had indeed come upon me again; I was interceding late into the nights. I did not sleep for the first several nights as I was constantly being led to intercede from late evening until the sun rose in the morning.

On the second night of the mission, I was praying when the Lord impressed upon me to walk out into the garden. Although I was fearful to leave the relative safety of my room and venture out into the dark African night, I was obedient to do so. I began to walk in a circle 40 feet in diameter and pray in the Spirit in the center of the hotel's garden and lawn. It was about 2 A.M. when I began to intercede. As I prayed, the Kingdom of Heaven began to manifest. I began to smell the familiar fragrance of frankincense floating around me in the clear, crisp African air. I became lost in the presence of Jesus. The anointing and presence of the sweet Holy Spirit grew intense and tangible. It seemed that I could actually taste the fragrances that were swirling around me. My mouth was filled with a wonderful taste of honey and roses! (See Psalm 34:8.)

The next night I was praying in the Spirit when the Lord spoke to me to return to the garden. This was a welcome suggestion to me. I began again to walk in a 40-foot-wide circle and prayed in the Spirit. I was on the same spot at the center of the hotel's garden and lawn. Immediately the fragrance of frankincense began to swirl around me in the garden in the cool of the night. The presence of the Lord grew thick in the air, and the Lord spoke, "Worship me in the Spirit." So I began to sing in the Spirit as I walked and danced in the circle. Time seemed to pass unnoticed in the presence of the Lord as I sang and worshiped Jesus in the Spirit and in truth.

After a short time, I began to realize that I was not singing alone. A host of angelic voices had begun to accompany me as I sang. The fragrance and anointing of the Lord hung heavily in the crisp night air. Shortly after I began to hear the voices that were accompanying me, I also began to see the source of the voices. At first it was just a passing glimpse into the spirit, but I gradually recognized angels dancing and singing around the circumference of the circle with me! This filled my spirit with a great excitement, and I began to sing louder in the Spirit.

Soon I began to see the circle of angels very clearly. The angels were singing in perfect unison with me. As I danced in the circle, the angels danced in flowing motion along with me. It seemed that the angels knew exactly what I would speak even before the words I was singing in tongues would leave my lips. I was singing and dancing in perfect unison and harmony with the angels.

I was enamored with not only their appearance, but also the absolute beauty of their ethereal singing and voices. It was a truly enchanting segment of time. It seemed that time itself stood still as I worshiped Jesus in the circle of angels. I skipped and danced around the circle like a small child totally mesmerized with the supernatural events unfolding. It seemed that the whole world had passed away and I was in a vacuum of time and space which was rife with the presence and love of Jesus. He was very near. As I danced and sang in tongues, the angels also continued to dance and worship Jesus along with me.

At times, individual angels would smile or wink at me as I focused upon them individually. It was only when the birds began to sing along with the angels that I realized that the sun was again about to come up. I had been dancing with the angels worshiping Jesus for hours. Now God's very creation was eagerly joining the angels and me as we sang and worshiped Jesus in unison. I have never looked at songbirds in the same manner since that morning.

On the fourth night, I was eager to return to my own private worship team. I made my way to my secret place in the gardens at about 12:30 A.M. When I stepped into the circle, the tangible presence of God and the Holy Spirit were awaiting me. I fell to my knees and began to weep. I was overcome with the revelation of how precious this privilege was. I gave the Lord Jesus glory for all of the miracles I had witnessed the last three days as many blind were healed. I also gave the Lord praise for the ongoing creative miracle happening with Leonard who was growing a new eyeball. I lifted my hands to Heaven, and I stayed in this posture of praise for a long time.

My concentration was broken when I began to hear the angels singing. I looked up, and this night I only saw fleeting glimpses of the angels dancing, but I could hear them very clearly. I knew that it was time for me to join them and dance and sing in the Spirit. So I arose and began to dance and sing like a little child. The peace, pleasure, and presence of the Lord enveloped me like a waterfall. It filled me with the love of Jesus. Tears streamed from my eyes as I danced and leaped before the Lord, singing with all of my heart.

After about an hour, I suddenly noticed that the angels were once more visible to my naked eyes, and I began to smile and interact with them as we danced and sang. The angels in turn also recognized me and acknowledged me by winking, smiling, or waving. Somehow I had a knowing that something very special was about to transpire. Suddenly, the glory increased in the circle, and I fell upon my knees in worship with my hands lifted to Heaven. I was no longer able to sing or pray. It was then that I saw Him. Jesus had stepped into the circle of angels. He was smiling at me. The love of God washed over me in waves and billows. I could see the Lord's nail-scarred hands and feet, and I was once again reminded of the great love that He carried not only for me, but for all of humankind.

The angels continued to sing and dance in the circle praising the Lord. However, I remained upon my knees gazing up at Jesus. As He looked deeply into my eyes, I could feel His unfathomable love and compassion for the nation of Malawi. Somehow I knew that I was to be His hands to touch the people. I was to be His lips to speak to the people. I was to be His ambassador to the nation of Malawi and to many other nations in Africa. It was not as if Jesus spoke to me in an audible voice; rather, I had a sovereign knowing of what He was commissioning me to do. Jesus reached out with His right hand and gently placed it upon my shoulder. I knew that the Lord had blessed me and had in some supernatural way empowered me for a work of His choosing. I closed my eyes for a moment. When I opened my eyes again, Jesus was gone.

I realized that my life had been transformed in that garden in the cool of the night. I continued to kneel for a long time on the spot where I had encountered Jesus. Tears of thanksgiving and gratefulness freely rolled from my eyes and down my cheeks. Torrents of tears dripped from my chin to the ground pooling there in the garden. The voices of angels continued to fill my ears, and the glory of God continued to fill my heart. I was lost in the Spirit. I was somewhere between

Heaven and earth. Suddenly, I was jarred back to my carnal senses by a voice. One of the team members from the mission trip said, "Wow, I smell the fragrance of the Lord! What have you been doing here?"

I began to laugh uncontrollably and continued to weep steadily. It was about 4 A.M. It took a few minutes to stand on my feet. I told him that we should worship and pray. So he joined me as we danced and prayed in the Spirit around the circle of angels. After a short time, he said that he could sense that Jesus was nearby and also detected the presence of the angels. He was right on both accounts. We continued to pray until the sun began to rise.

ONE WORD FROM GOD
ALTERS YOUR DESTINY

The next night I returned to the garden and began to pray at/around midnight. Again I sensed that the angels were present and the fragrance of the Lord permeated the African night. The taste of honey invaded my taste buds. The presence of the Lord was again tangible as I prayed in the Spirit and walked in the circle. I had a knowing that the heavens were now open in this geographical location. There was free access into the realms of the heavens here. The angels joined me, and again we danced and worshiped Jesus for hours.

A quick glance at the time revealed that over three hours had passed. It was well past 3 A.M. Suddenly, I realized that Jesus was near. The Lord spoke one word to me. Jesus said, "Apply." I had an immediate revelation the Lord was speaking about a discipleship program. At that moment, I was unable to think or speak in the tangible presence of the Lord Jesus. I was only able to say, "Yes, Lord," and once again I found myself on my knees. Tears flowed from my eyes, running down my face and pooling on the ground in the circle of angels. I was in this state of ecstasy for a long time. Again it was the singing and chirping of the morning birds that brought me back to my carnal thoughts.

I returned to my room. I lay upon my bed and meditated in my heart upon the consequences of Jesus' command to "apply." I knew in my carnal mind that it would be impossible for me to be part of the discipleship program because I didn't have the money needed to pay for it. As I meditated upon these things, I had a knowing that the Lord would give me more revelation and guidance about what I would need to do when I traveled to Las Vegas the next week. Honestly, at that time I felt that it was totally impossible for me to join the discipleship program. I told Jesus, "If You want me to be part of that discipleship program, then You will have to make a way where there seems to be none." I "altared" my *destiny into the hands of God.*

I left Malawi with my mindset radically challenged again. I was now certain that angels were a vital part of God's Kingdom and that angels are active in the realms of earth today. There was no question that the Lord had used the healing angel that had been working with me and the team as we prayed for the blind. We will look at how God's angelic ministry played a crucial role in a creative miracle when we read about Leonard later in the book.

The angelic encounters that I experienced in Malawi only reinforced the visions and third-heaven encounters that

I had been experiencing for the past year or so. I now began to embrace the ministry of angels more aggressively. I began to pray and ask the Lord to reveal the truth of this aspect of His Kingdom to me. Again He was faithful, and I started to experience a rapid increase of angelic activity and ministry in my life.

I mentioned in the previously cited testimonies about how the Lord did indeed give me more revelation and guidance about what I would need to do when I traveled to Las Vegas. The Lord allowed me to work with the angel of provision to loose the necessary funds from the realms of Heaven to be manifested upon earth. To my amazement, I was also accepted to participate in the discipleship program 24 hours after the finances all came in. Not only had the angel of provision supernaturally helped manifest the $25,000, he had also worked to give me favor with the application process and ministry.

Jesus had begun to increase my faith and knowledge of how to co-labor with angels and to *"call those things that are not as though they are"* (see Rom. 4:17). I was beginning to understand how we can work with angels to release the answer and manifestation of prayer. Along the journey, the Lord had also started to instruct me how to partner with the Holy Spirit and healing angels as I prayed for the sick.

This will be an important aspect of angelic ministry in the coming season as global healing revivals are released. The Lord will accelerate this aspect of angelic ministry as ordinary people will become skilled at co-laboring with angels of healing to release the gifts of miracles and healings. We will examine some of the principles concerning co-laboring with angels to release healings and miracles in the next chapter.

Chapter 9

HEALING ANGELS APPEAR

There are a multitude of healing angels that are available to us at this hour. It is important to understand how healing angels work with people. In this chapter, we are going to start building a foundation. Later we will expand our scope to learn more about how healing angels work and co-labor with us. I have shared the testimony of how Jesus assigned a healing angel to me. Since then the Lord has helped me understand how to perceive when the angel is present and how to work with the angel to manifest Christ's Kingdom. That angel regularly helps us minister in healing.

We are going to examine numerous healing and miracle testimonies that involve healing angels. These testimonies of angelic ministry come from around the world. We will consider examples of angelic ministry that have come from many nations and several continents. However, we can only include a fraction of the healing and miracle testimonies from people in this first book.

Healing angels are actively ministering to people throughout the earth. As we look at these testimonies, you will be given glimpses into the way angels help people pray for healing and touch others who need healings and miracles. The Lord has healing angels that are assigned to you. These testimonies will encourage you and build your gift of faith to work with Jesus' healing angels.

ALBERTA, CANADA, JUNE 2004

Kathy and I were ministering at New Life Christian Fellowship in Alberta, Canada, in June 2004. In one service in the small city of Hannah, the healing angel paid us a visit. As a result, Jesus healed deafness and several other infirmities. In one instance, a person actually saw the angel and was able to describe how the angel assisted in the ministry of healing very clearly. I feel confident about her testimony as it is very similar to times when I have witnessed the angel manifest. Her testimony is also very similar to that of John MacGirvin, whom I trust very much.

The other thing that is interesting about her testimony is that I did not see, smell, or perceive the angel in this instance. However, I did feel the anointing for healing manifest in my left arm and hand as electricity or fire. Never once did I mention the angel or angels while I was speaking that Sunday. I was actually talking about helping orphans. That is another reason I believe that she had a legitimate open-eyed vision of the healing angel. Here is the testimony exactly as she gave it to us.

Today as you were ministering in our church, I saw an angel standing over you. This was the first time ever that I had an open-eyed vision of an angel. He was not hovering but standing. He was within reach; as I stood on my tip toes extending my open hand upward, I envisioned touching his face. I am guessing that he was about seven feet tall.

It all started at the beginning of the service when you blew from your mouth a gush of air onto the girl you were ministering to. The anointing of God fell, and the angel appeared. It was like the clap of thunder, and he appeared instantly. The snow-white feathers from his wings fluttered about, floating to the floor. As you ministered, he moved with your every move; he stood behind you, never in front or beside, always behind you. His wings moved ever so slightly as he moved with you. His arms seemed disconnected from his wings as his hands often would come down and touch you ever so gently on your shoulders for a short period of time.

I sensed at these moments that the anointing was increasing and what you were speaking was from the throne room of Heaven. As you began to minister and lay your hands on individuals, there were times when he would touch you and times he would just remain behind you looking or gazing upon you. I sensed that at the times he laid his hands at the sides of your shoulders, the healing power of God was touching those individuals, and at the times his hands reached down, I sensed in the spirit that those individuals did not receive. It was nothing that you did or did not do. It was simply the timing and preparation of those individuals' hearts. The angel never stopped smiling. He appeared to be well pleased with what was taking place, whether certain individuals received or not.

There was an incredible peace about this angel. The skin on his face appeared a few shades darker than your own skin. The fact that his garments and the feathers were so white may have made his face appear darker because his hands were as white as snow as well. His hair draped onto his shoulders with loose ringlets of curls. The color was a medium brown shade with light colored highlights throughout. These highlights once again may have been a reflection of the radiance that emanated from him. The light that radiated from him was not blinding but definitely intense. Somewhat like the noonday sun on a bright, clear day. More than noticing the color of his eyes or the shape of his nose, I was fixated on the contentment of his stature.

He always appeared to be very gentle. He never was moving too quickly or irrationally, but always in sync with you. I also sensed that the angel was a reflection of the character that you have a lot like your personality was reflected in and through him. He appeared committed to you and you alone in the work of God you are doing. What an awesome encounter! I've reflected on this time and time again throughout the days. It's one of those glimpses into heavenly experiences that leave you wondering more and more about the awesomeness of the Lord God Almighty!

—ANGIE and CRIS WARWICK
Hannah, Alberta, Canada

KANSAS CITY, 2006

In 2006, we were holding a healing school at Christ Triumphant Church in Kansas City. On the fourth day of the teaching as I was getting ready to walk into the service to conduct a session and then pray for deliverance, this same healing angel appeared. I had asked two of my good friends to join me in the green room to pray for my voice and strength. As John MacGirvin and Dave stood and prayed for me, I began to smell the fragrance of frankincense. At the same moment, I also began to feel electricity and tingling shoot up and down my left arm and hand. I knew that the angel had stepped in behind me. John was standing in front of me, and he was speaking and praying over me.

John has a very strong prophetic gifting and operates in the seer anointing at a very high level. When the angel stepped into the room, I opened my eyes to see if John would pick up on its presence. In about two seconds, I saw John's eyes pop open, and his face turned a little red.

He stopped praying and said, "An angel just stepped up behind you."

I asked John to tell me what the angel looked like.

"He is about eight feet tall; he has long, golden-blond hair and bright blue eyes; he is powerful. This one has on a white robe with a gold belt, and he is carrying a big two-edged sword. The Lord has sent him to help you to minister healing!"

We had a good laugh and went into the service with our angelic co-worker.

There were several notable miracles in the service. Jesus healed many that morning. One woman from Chicago had two large tumors disappear. One tumor was the size of an apple; the other was the size of a golf ball. Several others also had growths dissolve; deaf ears were opened; a number had the vision disorder called floaters healed. Many other healings also manifested. A number of the healings occurred without anyone touching those who received the healing or miracle. I considered this encounter important because I trust John's ability to see into the spirit. When John explained how the angel looked, he described the angel's appearance exactly as I have seen the angel before. John's description matched how the angel appeared the first time I saw him and as he appeared at other times and places. Many others have seen this angel in healing services. This angel seems to follow us around the earth!

GOD USES HEALING ANGELS

God still uses healing angels today to minister to people. Jesus is the same yesterday, today, and forever. God is *Jehovah Rapha,* the God who heals you. Throughout recorded history, God has used countless saints in healings and miracles. Starting with the Israelites in Exodus 15:26, we see the Lord as a God of healing. *Jehovah Rapha* is the literal translation here that means, *"...I am the Lord who heals you."* The Lord has also used angels to minister or release healing to people on a regular basis.

We see an example of an angel used in the healing ministry in John 5:2-4:

> *Now there is in Jerusalem by the Sheep Gate a pool, which is called in Hebrew, Bethesda, having five porches. In these lay a great multitude of sick people, blind, lame, paralyzed, waiting for the moving of the water. For an angel went down at a certain time into the pool and stirred up the water; then whoever stepped in first, after the stirring of the water, was made well [healed] of whatever disease he had* (John 5:2-4).

The Greek word translated in this passage, *"was made well,"* is *hugies.*[1] This word means "to be made well, healthy, whole or true; to be rendered sound, whole, or to have total health." This passage refers to an angel that brings, imparts, or releases physical body healing. A great multitude of people were lying by the pool of Bethesda, and there were many healed in that place by the healing angel. We do not know from Scripture how frequently the healing angel would stir the water. However, I believe that we can safely infer that the healings occurred at regular intervals; otherwise, the pool of Bethesda would not have been crowded.

If I was one of those sick people who waited at the pool, I would have just soaked in the water continuously until the angel showed up and stirred the water. The description of the sick at the pool seems to indicate that they all waited on the perimeter of the pool; perhaps the angel would not manifest and release healing unless the pool was empty? It is possible that the Lord required an act of faith from the individual being healed, such as paying close attention to the waters and then making a decision to get wet, or make the plunge.

Often the Lord will require us to perform an act of obedience to receive from the realms of Heaven. This can be true for miracles and healings, but this can also be true when it comes to having our eyes opened to see into the realms of the spirit. Let's investigate a few more modern-day testimonies of healing angels from around the earth as we continue to learn how to partner with angels to loose the Kingdom of Heaven. It is important to remember that at times the Lord will require us to perform a prophetic act of obedience that will release the Kingdom of Heaven and allow us to see the angels that are already working around each of us.

ENDNOTE

1. "Hugies"; see http://www.studylight.org/lex/grk/view.cgi ?number=5199.

Chapter 10

WORKING WITH HEALING ANGELS

SINGAPORE, 2006

We were invited to the Church of Our Savior in Singapore in October 2006. We were asked to minister at three healing services on October 28 and 29. During the healing services on Saturday, I sensed the presence of an angel as Kathy and I prayed for the sick. At one point, I felt electricity shoot up and down my arm, and there was a powerful release of the healing anointing. We saw the Lord open deaf ears, and several people had vision healings. There were many other healings in the first two meetings.

The first healing service on Saturday was a bilingual English/Chinese service. Before the service, the Lord told me that He was going to do something powerful. I preached about simple faith for salvation and for healing. The sermon was translated into Mandarin. I felt that there was some difficulty in the translation, so I spoke a little "heart prayer" something like this: "Oh, Jesus, I don't think I am getting through. I need Your help."

Suddenly I felt a wind blow into the sanctuary and knew that an angel had stepped into the meeting. For a fleeting moment, I saw a large angel at the rear of the auditorium. He was perhaps 40 feet tall. I could not see him clearly but perceived a faint outline of where he stood. I could see that he had his wings spread out. They covered nearly one third of the width of the edifice. He was tall enough that his upper body reached well above the second-level balcony section, and I could sense that his wings were gently flapping as I spoke.

Near the end of the sermon, the angel began to move his wings more quickly as I gave an invitation to come to the altar to receive Jesus as Savior. I perceived the angel "flapping" his wings over the congregation again. At first no one moved, but when the angel began to move his wings, I started to feel the "wind of his wings" that reached the platform. At that moment, people got up to come to the altar from the large congregation. Suddenly there were dozens of people coming from all over the sanctuary. The angel continued to "minister to the people with his wings." People continued to come forward for salvation until there were dozens of people at the altar.

As I began to lead the new converts in the prayer of salvation, I happened to glance back at the area where I had first seen the angel. For an instant, I could clearly see that he had stopped moving or fluttering his wings, and he was standing with his arms crossed over his chest and smiling at the results of the altar call. Later, one of the pastors told me that some pastors were quite surprised that so many people had received Jesus. They had thought that the message I had preached was almost "too simple," and had not expected to have a large response. Some of the people who had been saved that evening had been attending church for years, yet had never received salvation. They had heard hundreds of messages about salvation, yet had never come forward. I just smiled as the pastor shared this with me. I knew that it was not my ability to preach but an anointing that the heavenly visitor released into the meeting.

I am not certain what was taking place as the angel created a "wind of the Spirit" as he flapped his wings over the sanctuary. Perhaps he was releasing the glory of God into the meeting. It is possible that under God's glory the people suddenly realized their sinful nature and responded to the simple message of salvation for the spirit, soul, and body. I know that it was their personal decision to come to the altar to receive Christ as Savior. Perhaps the angel that I saw was one like John saw in Revelation 14:6: *"Then I saw another angel flying in the midst of heaven, having the everlasting gospel to preach to those who dwell on the earth—to every nation, tribe, tongue, and people."* I have often wondered if this was an angel that was assigned to Asia or to Singapore. Here is Pastor Christian Chia's testimony about the events that transpired in Singapore in 2006.

> ***Greetings from Singapore!*** I am pleased to confirm that, coincidentally, a few other guest preachers have also reported seeing "healing" or other angels in our church. I personally was

not able to see the angel you have mentioned on this occasion. But I can testify that an unusually large number of people came forward to the altar for ministry by you and Kathy. During each of the three healing services over that weekend, scores of people came forward to the altar with various needs. Altogether, a few hundred people had received ministry. Many pre-believers received *Jesus* as their personal Savior and Lord! Many more experienced healings and miracles! The presence of the Holy Spirit was powerful! All glory to our Lord *Jesus*!

—CHRISTIAN CHIA
Church of Our Saviour, Singapore

Later, I discerned that an angel was in the sanctuary, although I did not see him. Nevertheless, I did feel the anointing on my hands and left arm. At one point in the healing ministry, the angel whispered into my left ear, and I was able to call a woman out by name in Chinese. Although I do not speak that language, this "Chinese word of knowledge" turned out to be accurate. The woman was healed.

Later still, I was instructed to ask for eight women who had one leg shorter than the other. We asked them to sit in a row of chairs, and during prayer, each of their legs grew out one by one. Most notable, one leg grew out about 2 inches, and the others also grew various lengths. This sparked the faith of the people. The Lord healed others of deafness, chronic sinusitis, tumors, and many other infirmities. We also ministered prophetically to hundreds of saints. Kathy and I experienced supernatural strength and prayed for hours. These kinds of angelic interventions continued to rearrange our mindset concerning angels who are involved in the healing ministry and evangelism. It seems that the more that Kathy and I embrace angelic ministry, the more it increases in intensity. Embracing angels is an important key and one of the first steps to working with angels.

DENTIST ANGEL

We have a friend who carries a powerful healing anointing. Dave shared a testimony about a healing angel that is quite amazing. Dave had been called by a friend who was suffering with an abscessed and painful toothache. Dave agreed to pray for the person. They had been sitting in the living room and prayed for the toothache several times; however, there seemed to be little effect from the intense prayer ministry. Dave is persistent when it comes to praying for the sick, but after several different approaches and attempts to heal this stubborn toothache, they had seen no real result, and the man's tooth seemed to ache all the more.

In a bit of frustration, Dave released what I call a "heart's prayer" and thought, *Lord, I think that I am going to need some help on this one.* A moment later Dave said that he saw a man walk "through the front door." The angel did not open the door, but rather passed through the material of the door, stepping into the hallway and walking right up to the man with the toothache. Dave said that he saw the angel quite clearly and described his attire to me. The angel was wearing blue jeans, tennis sneakers, and a flannel shirt. The angel touched the man's jaw and simply turned around and just disappeared. Instantly the man's toothache was healed. Sometimes when we ask for help, the Lord responds with angels! Asking is another important and simple key to working with angels.

PERU, 2004

There have been a few times when I have seen angels materialize and touch those who were being healed just like the last testimony. One of the first times that I witnessed an angel of healing ministering to an individual was in a small city in Peru in 2004. During that service I was preaching from John 5. During a time of prayer prior to the service, the Holy Spirit told me to preach from John 5 because He wanted to show me something new. I was given instructions to prophesy that the Lord was going to release an anointing into the church like that of John 5. I was instructed by the Holy Spirit to tell the pastor and the congregation that many would come to the altar there and receive healing as the result of an angel of healing that the Lord would release to minister in the church, just like in John 5.

I began to preach in this manner, and according to what I had "seen" in prayer. I also poured a generous amount of anointing oil on the altar. I poured this oil in the exact spot that I had seen in a vision while I was in prayer prior to the meeting that Sunday morning. This was another prophetic act of obedience. I continued to preach from John 5, and after a few minutes, an elderly woman stood up and slowly walked to the spot at the altar where I had poured the anointing oil.

As I glanced up from the Scriptures to see her approaching the altar, I noticed two things.

The first thing I saw was that she was powerfully under the influence of the Holy Spirit. Tears of joy were streaming from her eyes. The next thing I saw astonished me, and I was filled with a great faith for the miraculous to break into the meeting. On the spot where I had anointed the altar there stood a large angel. He stood about 9 feet tall.

The angel was not transparent as some I had seen in the past; rather, this angel was "full bodied," or solid looking. This experience would be classified as an open-eyed angelic encounter. When the elderly woman came within arm's length of the angel, he reached out with both of his hands and gently touched her eyes! Instantly the woman shrieked and fell to the floor. When the woman fell to the floor, the angel bent over her and began to slowly rub his hands over her eyes.

I continued to preach from John 5 as the woman lay on the floor with the angel ministering to her. Shortly after that, the woman began to stir and blink her eyes. She began to weep loudly, and streams of tears were rolling from her eyes. She shouted something in Spanish. I asked the pastor to get her testimony. I was anxious to hear what she would say after I had seen the angel ministering to her for the past several minutes. At first the woman could not stop weeping, and I was told by the interpreter that she kept screaming, "I can see, praise God, I can see again. I can see you all!"

A little later, the elderly woman shared her testimony about what she had just experienced. She told the church that she had witnessed the angel enter the church through the ceiling and stand at the altar. She decided to "be the first one in the water" because she understood that the angel healed the first one in the water at the Pool of Bethesda. That is when she walked up to the angel that she was seeing at the altar, and he had touched her eyes.

These testimonies demonstrate how angels can affect the environment and can be used to release salvation, healing, and miracles. As we have ministered around the world, we have frequently had people come to us and share about how they have seen an "angel or angels" around Kathy and me as we have ministered. Once in London a man stopped me in the street and said, "I'm not sure if you know it, but I thought you should know that there is a big angel walking behind you with its wings spread over your shoulders."

Actually I was aware of the angel's presence, but it was very interesting to have someone tell me about his company. We have entered into a season when many ordinary people will begin to see angels as they are moving about our world. Later we will look at some important principles that can help you activate your ability and gifting to see angels. It is important to realize that when you begin to see angels, that is only the first step into the Kingdom of Heaven. The Lord has a purpose for His angels and for allowing you to see them.

Chapter 11

HEALING ANGELS IN REDDING, CALIFORNIA

Kathy and I were in Redding, California, to attend a conference at Bethel Church in 2004. We had also been invited to speak at the Church of the Redeemed. I was praying in Pastor Tim Moore's office and waiting on the Lord. I locked the door and purposed in my heart that unless the Holy Spirit gave me some direction for the service, I would just stay in the office all morning. I never did get any direction. Finally the worship stopped, and I could hear Pastor Tim speaking, but I continued to lay on the floor waiting on the Lord. Finally there was a knock at the door, and I was asked to come and speak. I did not feel prepared when I walked into the service.

I did not have any leading as to what the Lord wanted me to say or how I was to minister. The reason for this became very clear in about two minutes. I was just about to share my testimony when I suddenly felt the anointing and fire began to shoot through my left arm and hand. I realized that an angel had just stepped into the room, and I realized the Lord had something else in mind. I sensed that this was the same angel that I had been seeing in other healing services. I thought, *Lord, what do You want me to do here?*

The Holy Spirit said, "The angel is here to help you pray for the deaf and the others who need a miracle in this place."

So I stopped in mid-sentence saying, "If you're here today and you have deafness or partial deafness, come to the front, and the Lord is going to heal you!" I was surprised to see seven people come to the front. When I stepped up to pray for the people, the angel moved to stand behind me. As I placed my hand on the people's ears, I could feel the angel place his hands on my shoulders.

The angel did not always use both hands. Sometimes he only put one hand on my shoulder, and at other times he would put two. When the angel stepped up behind me, I could feel a power, or electricity, course through my left arm and the hair on my body stood on end. It felt like someone placed a full-length fur coat over my body—except the coat was electrified. We prayed for every deaf ear, and Jesus opened them all. Some were only partially deaf. Others were totally deaf in one ear, and their deaf ear was completely restored according to their testimonies. We continued to pray for several others. Several with vision impairments were touched and reported that they could see well after prayer. I continued to pray for the sick for the remainder of the service. After about 40 minutes, the electricity seemed to fade, and I knew that the angel had stepped out of the church.

I found it most comforting that the Lord sent the angel when I felt the weakest and most unprepared. Remembering that the Holy Spirit was not giving me any direction or Scriptures to use was actually the Lord's way of saying that He had a better plan. So again, this was a learning process. We were beginning to understand how the Holy Spirit and angelic ministry work in symphony. The angel was obviously sent to release healing to the people. At this meeting, I began to understand that this angel was going to travel with Kathy and me consistently as we ministered in various places.

HEALING TESTIMONIES

Here is Pastor Tim Moore's testimony of the healings that happened that day in Redding:

> Thank you so much for coming to Redeemed. The Lord, through many healings of deafness and eye dysfunctions, confirmed that your ministering here was a real faith builder for our congregation. We are excitedly waiting for more testimonies that we know are coming. We hope that you will be back in California in the near future. You are welcome to come back to the Redeemed anytime. You and Kathy have blessed us here.
>
> —PASTOR TIM MOORE, Senior Pastor
> Church of the Redeemed
> Redding, California

Another interesting testimony came from the Sunday morning service. Kathleen Loosli, from Wasilla, Alaska, was in town and felt that she was supposed to come to The Church of the Redeemed with Kathy and me. After the meeting, we discussed with Kathleen the healing angel that I had perceived and felt. She attended a service that night at Bethel Church in which Larry Randolph spoke. Just a few hours after the service at Redeemed, he prophesied about what we had just experienced. This really impacted Kathleen. She was very excited and sent us the following testimony:

> Well, I just wanted to let you guys know what happened after you went on to Sacramento. I went to the conference at Bethel Church and heard Larry Randolph. He was preaching and prophesying about a "Breaker Angel" that the Lord was releasing to the Northeast, and He talked all about angels. His message was amazing in light of what happened with you guys. He said that angels are going to start showing up at meetings regularly and that we (ordinary people) are going to be partnering with angels in ministry.
>
> He said that if we were able to humble ourselves and let the Holy Spirit come, people were not going to have to preach or talk...but that miracles would happen as we partner with angels. So I thought that is exactly what happened Sunday!

The Lord used Kathleen to help establish our faith concerning the angelic experiences we were beginning to walk in. Kathleen's email helped cement our mindsets in relation to the angel of healing that seems to follow us around! We began to embrace the fact that angels were constantly available to partner or co-labor with us as we minister. We have allowed our mindsets to become open to the fact that angels are not only available but enthusiastic about working alongside us. As a result, we immediately saw a dramatic increase in miracles and healings that Jesus worked in our lives as we exercised our spiritual senses to embrace angelic ministry. You can too. Working with healing angels is really quite simple.

SOUTHWEST VIRGINIA

Next we were scheduled to travel to southwest Virginia. We had been contacted by a local pastor there to meet with us. At this point I was on fire in terms of praying for healing. We ministered in his church, and as we called out words of knowledge for healing, several people responded and were touched by the Holy Spirit, testifying to being healed. That was the reason they wanted us to come in the first place.

After I had prayed for about four people, I suddenly smelled frankincense, and the hair on my left arm became electrified. I could feel the presence of the healing angel behind me. I was certain that the same angel of healing that was just in Redding had followed us. I "knew" that I was to call for the deaf and partially deaf people to come to the platform. I was surprised to see seven deaf or partially deaf people come up for prayer. As I prayed for them, I could feel the healing angel place his hand on my shoulder, and each one in turn was healed as we laid hands on them.

There was one man, Karl Pennington, who received a creative miracle. He did not have an opening where his right ear was, and was totally deaf in that ear from birth—50 years. I had witnessed a young boy named James Joseph who had a similar condition of deafness receive a creative miracle in Tanzania. An ear hole just seemed to appear as we prayed for James, and he was able to hear. So I had confidence that the Lord would do a similar miracle for Karl.

I began to pray the words that the angel whispered into my left ear. As I prayed, I felt a sensation of popping hit my left hand which was on his right ear. It seemed that a waxy gooey substance blew out of his ear and hit my hand. I asked Karl what had happened, and he said that he was beginning to hear in his right ear.

"I thought you were completely deaf in that ear," I said.

"I was!" We prayed for Karl several times, and he began to hear progressively better until he was hearing well.

This was a true creative miracle, and he was hearing quite well for the first time in his life out of his right ear! I am sure God's angel that was standing behind me played a role in this creative miracle. Karl later told me that it was medically impossible for him to hear as he had been deaf from birth and had no "working parts" in his right ear. There was no eardrum, none of the tiny bones, not even an opening or ear canal. Here is Karl's testimony of the events of the night.

Kevin and Kathy prayed for me May 23, 2004. That night you prayed for seven people who had varying degrees of deafness. All of those people testified to being made whole. I was the last to be prayed for, and I was completely deaf in my right ear since birth—50 years ago. You prayed for me three or four times. Each time I began to hear a little better. Your wife Kathy also prayed for me. I could hear a little better after each time that you both prayed. I would estimate that I can hear about 30 percent. (That is pretty good for someone who was totally deaf!) I have never been able to hear out of this ear before as I have always been totally deaf from birth. As we drove home after the service, Cheryl asked me a question, and I answered her without turning my head. That is something that I have never been able to do since we were married. I am now hearing out of my right ear for the first time since birth! Praise God!

This is the second time that you and your wife have prayed for me and Cheryl, my wife; about three years before you had prayed for us in Bluewell at the Voice of Praise Church. You prayed for my shoulder joint and for Cheryl's back and a fatty tumor that she had. Both of us were healed that night and remain healed to this day. Her tumor is gone, and my shoulder has never hurt again from that night on. What I'd like to do is submit my testimony for the record—for those who do not receive their healing right away or have a creative miracle immediately.

—KARL PENNINGTON, DSS

MIRACLE EXPLOSION

There is an acceleration of creative, or "special miracles," that is taking place in the earth today. Actually, we have not seen very many creative miracles in contrast to other people that we know. These kinds of creative miracles should be common, and they will become widespread in the approaching global outpourings. Angels will play a key role in this phenomenon of creative, or special, miracles. Let's look at the rationale and explanation for the angel's involvement in special miracles in the next chapter.

Chapter 12

HEALING ANGELS AND THE MANTLE FOR CREATIVE MIRACLES

These next few testimonies illustrate how we can exercise our spiritual senses, and utilize the spiritual tools available to us to activate our ability to work with angels. We touched on these spiritual tools in Chapter 3, and we will look at them in greater depth in the coming pages. Keep this in mind as you read these testimonies.

Kathy and I have continued to press into the Lord during this time frame, seeking more creative miracles. At times, the Lord releases healing angels with the ability to help people manifest creative miracles like Karl's. Certain angels carry an individual anointing for specific types of miracles. Some angels are empowered by the Lord to heal deaf ears, for example. Other angels may be empowered to release creative miracles like growing eyeballs or other missing body parts. The Lord can dispatch these special miracle angels to the place where a specific miracle is needed to be released to a particular individual.

Several supernatural experiences that I had in 2001 and 2002 underscore this belief. On one occasion, Jesus invited me into the realms of Heaven much as He had done previously. In one of those visions, the Lord took me into His library. We sat in front of a large fireplace and fellowshipped. While we were speaking, there were several strong angels who stood around us in the sitting room. I also observed many vaults nearby in this heavenly place. On another occasion, I was able to investigate one vault that contained millions upon millions of rare books.

Jesus Himself guided me into that vault full of books. He led me to a very special book. I was able to read "the book of life" that belongs to my daughter Miranda. I read through the pages until she was nine years old, and at that moment I could not bear to look any further. So I returned her book of life to the shelf. Yet another time I saw a vault that contained spare body parts. This room had countless hearts, livers, eyeballs, fingers, arms, and many other body parts neatly arranged upon shelves. These "spares" were in the charge of several strong angels. These angels seemed to be milling around and waiting for an opportunity to "go to work." When I walked into the room, they looked at me with great excitement and anticipation. These angels are anxiously awaiting us to put them to work or assign them to missions of mercy.

On another occasion, while I was in the sitting room, Jesus instructed two angels to take me into another large vault. This vault was massive. It was similar to a bank vault with a large door. The vault seemed to be endless, and the ceiling was about 50 feet tall. Both sides of the vault were lined with shelves. The vault also had rolling ladders, much like you might see in a library, on either side of the walls.

The two angels took me in, and I was allowed to look at the contents of the vault. The shelves were lined with thousands upon thousands of neatly wrapped boxes. Clearly the contents of the boxes had been stored in this place with great care. What they contained was obviously very valuable. I took the time to examine many of them. There were boxes of many different shapes and sizes. Soon I noticed that each box had a name inscribed on the golden surface. I did not recognize the vast majority of the names inscribed on the beautiful boxes. However, I did recognize Smith Wigglesworth and Maria Woodworth-Etter, to name a couple. My mind began to race as I contemplated what the boxes contained.

Suddenly one of the boxes seemed to emit a supernatural light, and I was attracted to it. One of the angels indicated that I could have any box that I wished. I took the phosphorescent box in my hands. When I touched it, I felt the power and anointing of the Holy Spirit course through my hands. As I opened the box, I realized that it contained the mantle of Stephen. The angels gently removed the article of clothing from the container and placed the mantle upon me. It was loose fitting and was very comfortable on me, sort of like a one-size-fits-all garment. I returned to the sitting room still wearing the mantle. Jesus was patiently waiting for me. The Lord looked at me, noted the mantle that I was wearing, and said, "You have chosen well." Jesus walked over to me and placed His hands upon my shoulders. He smiled at me and said, "Well done."

As Jesus placed His hands upon my shoulders, I received revelation. The Lord is releasing the anointing of the gift of faith and the power to work great wonders and miracles back into the earth. One of many ways this will be accomplished will be the result of the ministry of strong angels like the two angelic beings that I saw in the vaults. We are entering into a time when unusual miracles, or what some describe as creative miracles or special miracles, will be released and orchestrated with the help of angelic ministry. This kind of angelic help is accessible to ordinary people today. The mantle of Stephen is available to you at this hour (see Acts 6:8).

ANGELS IN AFRICA

In 2003, on my third trip to Africa, I traveled to South Africa and Malawi. I was leading teams into the hospitals, streets, clinics, and at crusade outreaches. This trip was high-lighted by a visitation of Jesus that I described in Chapter 9. Prior to the trip, I was in Kansas City, Missouri. I had invested five days at the International House of Prayer. I stayed at the International House of Prayer for about 120 hours fasting and praying about the trip to Malawi. I prayed in the Spirit and drank from the worship—and the water fountain in the hall—as I waited on the Lord. At that time, there was a room dedicated to praying for Africa. I invested a lot of time praying over the map of Africa there.

As I prayed, it was as if the heavens were brass over my head (see Deut. 28:23). I just could not get a breakthrough into the realms of Heaven to hear clearly from the Lord. That is one reason I ended up a little over five days in a row in the prayer room. I purposed in my heart that I was not going to leave until I got a word from Heaven. After about 72 hours, the Lord told me to read Acts 4. So I began to read Acts 4. I must have read Acts 4 hundreds of times. However, I was not getting any "real revelation" from my exercise.

By fasting and praying over the Scriptures, I had begun to knock and ask the Lord to release the revelation that I was sure Jesus had for me in the fourth chapter of Acts. I would read the chapter and ask the Lord, "OK, Jesus, what do You want me to see?" After reading it constantly for about three days in a row, the Lord finally said, "Look at verses 29 and 30!"

I gave a big sigh. I had read Acts 4:29-30 hundreds of times already, and there was just no oil coming from the Rock. Those verses tell us,

Now, Lord, look on their threats, and grant to Your servants that with all boldness they may speak Your word, by stretching out Your hand to heal, and that signs and wonders may be done through the name of Your holy Servant Jesus (Acts 4:29-30).

"OK, Jesus," I said, "what is it about these two Scripture verses that You want me to see?"

The Holy Spirit said, "Read them again."

So I invested about another 24 hours reading Acts 4:29-30 over and over again. By now I had been at the International House of Prayer for about 100 hours and was in need of a real shower. I must have read Acts 4:29-30 a thousand times by now. Then the Lord said, "Look at the Scripture again." So I did. Again I was obedient to the Holy Spirit's leading and combined prayer, fasting, and meditating upon God's Word in this season.

That is when I saw it. Boldness! Yes, that was the oil! The morning star had arisen in my heart, and I had the revelation! Boldness: *"...with all **boldness** they may speak Your word, by stretching out Your hand to heal, and that signs and wonders may be done through the name of Your holy Servant Jesus."* The Lord has given His children the authority to pray with all boldness in His name! All boldness is in the name of Jesus Christ! In an instant, the penny dropped, and Acts 4:29-30 became sharp and alive in my spirit, soul, and body. It became the Living Word; it became a *rhema* to me.

The Lord began to encourage me to believe Him for creative miracles while I was in Africa. He wanted me to believe for missing fingers and toes to grow back as we pray with boldness in His mighty name! He wanted me to believe for the dead to be raised as we pray with boldness in His mighty name! (Incidentally, it was on this trip that Sammy Robinson and I "broke into the morgue" to pray for the dead in Lilongwe. But I won't go into that!) God had birthed in me a holy hunger and passion to work creative miracles as I pray with boldness in His mighty name! Of course! I was ready to see the dead rise. I was expecting to see a lot of creative miracles. I had somehow been given a "gift of faith" for the miraculous! I left the House of Prayer on fire! (I may have smelled like it too!) By the time we arrived in Malawi, I had continued to meditate on Jesus working with me and was asking God to release creative miracles as we prayed with boldness in His mighty name!

THE BLIND LEADING THE BLIND

Part of my duties as a team leader was to load up the mission team members into vans for the drive from the airport. By now everyone was very tired from the long flight, but we were very excited to be on the ground again! Oh, how I do love the smell of Africa! I got a group into a twelve-seat bus, and we took off for the hotel. Everyone was talking and very exuberant for the mission. The driver took off like a shot. Since I had been to East Africa before, his erratic driving did not concern me. I was on the left front seat and noticed that the woman right behind me was holding on to the bar between the seats for dear life! Her knuckles were white, and her eyes were popping out a bit. At that moment a huge Mercedes semi truck and our van had a very close call; we narrowly missed a collision. There was a simultaneous shriek from the whole team.

I thought that our driver might have had a nip or two, so I tugged on his left sleeve to see if I could tell if he had been drinking. When he turned toward me, I noticed that he did not have a right eyeball. I screamed to the people in the van, "Don't worry, he isn't drunk! He's only blind!" That observation did not go over too well or help relieve their concern!

The driver, Leonard, had an infected-looking opening where an eyeball should have been. There was no prosthetic eye. The socket looked like it had an angry infection, and there was crust around its perimeter. Immediately the Holy Spirit reminded me of the Lord's promise to work with me as

I prayed with *all boldness* in His mighty name! I explained to the team that Leonard had only one eye, hoping to sooth their concern. One of the ladies told the driver that this preacher had seen eyes grow back and that he would be in Malawi in two days.

I stopped her and said, "Hey, Leonard, I have a better idea; how about we pray for your eye to grow back when we get to the hotel?" Leonard liked that idea better! When we reached the hotel, I laid my hands on Leonard's eye socket, and Shara, a young woman from the team, and I began to pray for him. As we prayed with *all boldness* commanding an eye to form, an ugly, foul-smelling, white liquid began to weep from his eye socket.

Leonard was really drunk now, not on whiskey as we first thought, for the Holy Spirit was filling him. He was smiling as the anointing washed through him. I felt a now-familiar presence behind me, and the healing angel whispered into my left ear. I would just pray what he whispered. When I took my hand away after boldly commanding "an eye to form," there was what appeared to be a small "white seed" of an eye in his once-empty socket. When I removed my hand, Leonard said, "I do see some light." The seed was about the size of a BB. This testimony is a great example of how people can work with the anointing of the Holy Spirit in concert with healing angels to manifest the gifts of the Spirit.

The next day Leonard was waiting for me at the Sunbird Capitol Hotel. He had made an agreement with the other bus drivers that a certain *wuzungo,* or white man, would be riding with him. Leonard had been touched by the anointing, and he realized that his miracle had started. Leonard wanted more prayer. We laid hands on him a second time and prayed with *all boldness* in Jesus' mighty name. Once again, I could feel the heat and electricity as it manifested in my left arm and hand as I commanded the eye to grow. The angel was near again. Several team members joined in the prayer. Again, when I removed my hand, I could see Leonard's fresh new eye. It was about the size of a pea by now.

Leonard smiled, telling the team he could now see light and shadows. After more prayer, Leonard told me that he could see a "fuzzy outline" of my hand (like the blind man in Mark 8:22-26 who saw men walking as trees). The next morning Leonard was at the hotel waiting for the team. He was growing hungry for his miracle, and the Lord was continuing to release boldness in the team. My team had already seen over one dozen totally blind people healed as we had ministered in various outreaches in the city. A gift of faith for the blind to see had blossomed in me after I saw Leonard's "eye seed" beginning to grow.

The next day Leonard sought me out to pray for his growing eyeball for the third consecutive day. By now Leonard's new eye was about the size of a small marble. Leonard was laughing and praising God for his new eye. What's more, he was beginning to see more clearly with his new eye! The angel would step near and whisper into my left ear. I was becoming comfortable with the fire in my left hand as I prayed for the blind. I would pray the words I heard and, *wham!* On almost every occasion, the blind person would immediately begin to see. Amazing—this ministry of God's healing angels!

By now Leonard was becoming a sort of celebrity among the 100-member mission team. A lot of people wanted to see the "man who was growing a new eye." That day, June 6, 2003, the teams were feeding the poor in a large refugee camp. This was big news, and a reporter and cameraman from the regional television station were on the scene filming the distribution of the corn and rice that were being given away.

I was surprised when the reporter came looking for me. It seemed that they were also filming testimonies of the various miracles that God was doing. They wanted me to introduce them to the "man who was growing the eye." Leonard was not around, so they settled for talking to me. Here I was in Malawi, and I was speaking about Jesus and His working with us as we prayed with *all boldness* in His mighty name. I got to preach on television a short sermon about God's power to heal!

That night at the crusade meeting Leonard was invited onto the platform to share his testimony. Leonard's new eye was now about the size of a regular glass marble. The preacher asked Leonard to test his new eye by covering his good eye. Leonard was able to see more clearly. He was able to identify a Bible, a pair of glasses, and finally a small Life Saver candy!

The next morning Leonard was ready to have more prayer. I checked his new eye; it was about the size of a grape, and an iris and pupil had started to form. We prayed for him again, and it appeared that his eye seemed to grow a little more. Leonard told me that he was "seeing better" with his new eye, but that he wanted more prayers, because he desired "perfect sight" with his new eye. Now that is faith! Leonard's determination is an example for those who are in need of a miracle.

During the outreach that day, a cameraman from the national television station came to us and asked if he could interview Leonard to get his testimony. He asked Leonard to share his testimony with the nation of Malawi! I was also interviewed along with Leonard on national television. We prayed for Leonard three more days, and each day his eye grew a bit more.

The last time I saw Leonard's new eye, it was nearly normal in size, and he was seeing very well according to his testimony. By then, it was easy to see the new pupil and iris. Leonard's creative miracle triggered many more healings while I was in Africa. While the team was in Malawi, I witnessed 62 blind people healed; when we went to South Africa, we saw 10 more blind people healed. I witnessed 72 people having blind eyes opened.

During one outreach to a refugee camp, a team member received a word of knowledge and went to the translator and told the village to "bring all of your blind people to the people under the trees, and Jesus will heal them." As the team of eight prayed, we witnessed 42 blind eyes opened in about 45 minutes! I feel certain that a healing angel was standing in the midst of the prayer team that afternoon. When one of these healing angels arrives, anyone who is ministering nearby will see powerful miracles and healings as they pray with *all boldness* in the mighty name of Jesus.

A PROCESS

Another thing that I learned during this season was that creative miracles can at times be a process. Sometimes the miracle manifests over an extended period of time. It is important to understand this principle whether you are praying for miracles or are seeking to receive a creative miracle. Sometimes miracles and healings are given as seeds and do not occur immediately. However, if you are healed in one minute or in one week, the end result is the same. I discovered in my experience of praying for Leonard's creative miracle that even though the healing angel was present, when we prayed, the angel's presence did not guarantee an instant result. You should keep this in mind as you begin to work with God's angels.

Creative miracles will become quite common in the coming season. We have witnessed many creative miracles over the past few years in association with visitations of healing angels. We will begin to witness a miracle explosion throughout the earth. The Lord will accelerate the release of the mantle for creative miracles. One of the tools the Lord will use to establish this is angelic ministry. Creative miracles will begin to flourish, and many people will be brought into the Kingdom of Heaven as a result. Remember to pray with "all boldness" in the mighty name of Jesus Christ of Nazareth (see John 17:1-10).

The most exciting aspect of this imminent release of the mantle for "creative and unusual miracles" is that this ability is available to all of us. The Lord will begin to work through ordinary people to accomplish these kinds of special miracles at this hour. Angels with the mantle and anointing for creative miracles will be assigned to people throughout the earth. You can step into the mantle for these types of creative miracles. Anyone can work with angels today. The Lord's healing angels are waiting for you and me to activate them through the Holy Spirit in the mighty name of Jesus Christ. The next chapter sums up a few of the easy methods that you can implement to activate angelic ministry in your life.

Chapter 13

ACTIVATING ANGELIC ENCOUNTERS IN YOUR LIFE

As we have pressed in to understand various aspects of working with the Lord's angels, Kathy and I have found that most biblical and modern angelic encounters have similar characteristics. Understanding these similarities can activate angelic help and intervention in our lives. We are not suggesting that every person will encounter angels. However, we do believe that angelic ministry and help will be available to a vastly increased number of individuals in the coming days. The ability to recognize angels and work with them will not be limited to a few "chosen vessels" any longer.

We have entered a *kairos* moment of time. Our omnipresent God has chosen you to be alive at this exact moment of time. The inhabitants of Heaven are very excited about the imminent release of the angelic invasion that is being revealed and loosed for us to employ at this hour.

We will see pandemics, financial turmoil, and great natural disasters. Earthquakes, pestilences, famines, wars, and rumors of wars will spread across the face of the earth. Darkness and evil will greatly increase. Humankind will call good evil and evil good. However, in the midst of these horrible and dark times, the glory of our God will arise upon His people. The Lord will empower regular people to interact with His Kingdom and the angels therein.

For those who are friends of God, these times will be times of great anointing, power, and remarkable blessing. Many will grow to know Jesus and experience a wonderful intimacy with God. They will abide under the shadow of His wings, and no evil shall befall them. They will walk in a demonstration of God's miracle-working power. They will minister under the anointing and direction of the Holy Spirit. One other small but important supernatural weapon that these ordinary people will have at their disposal is the ability to activate angelic ministry. Let's summarize several keys that can help you activate this supernatural weapon in your life. In this chapter we will look at eight basic keys that can be helpful to activating angelic ministry in your life.

PRAYER AND PRESSING IN

We have seen from both our modern-day testimonies and from biblical examples that angels are often released and encountered in response to the prayers of people. Prayer that is accompanied by fasting and meditating upon God's Word seems to accelerate the ministry of angels in a person's life. It has been my experience that as we entertain angels they seem to manifest more readily. As we violently and relentlessly press in to God's Kingdom with prayer, fasting, and meditating upon God's Word, angels will begin to "hang around." At times it is necessary to militantly take the kingdom of God by force. During these times as we entertain angels, they will become more noticeable to us. The ability to see or discern angels is only the entry point into this aspect of Jesus' Kingdom (see Matt. 11:12).

Entertaining angels is a very important phase of pressing into the Kingdom and seeking to understand how to work with angels. Really, it boils down to simply asking the Lord to allow you to interact with angels according to the principle found in Matthew 7:7: *"Ask, and it will be given to you; seek, and you will find; knock, and it will be opened to you."* As simple as this may sound, one of the most important keys to activating angelic ministry and encounters in your life may be asking. When we ask our heavenly Father for the spiritual aspects of His Kingdom, Jesus promised us that we will receive them.

OPEN HEAVENS

At times as we earnestly press in to the Kingdom with prayer, fasting, and meditation on God's Word, we can create a "thin spot" in the spiritual atmosphere over our lives. Some people call this phenomenon an "open heaven." There are certain geographic locations throughout the earth where the heavens are activated or open. We also see two such places in Genesis 32:1-2 and Genesis 28:10-12. Jacob called the name of that first place *Mahanaim*, or "camp of God." Jacob also encountered a "thin" place near Haran where he "saw" angels ascending and descending to and from Heaven. These kinds of places are still available today.

Jesus Himself spoke of places where there are open heavens. At times the heavens can be opened over an individual as well as a geographic place. One easy way to activate your eyes to see into the realm of angels is to go to a place where the heavens are already open. When you find an open heaven, you will also find angelic movement and activity. When you come into a place like this, a *Mahanaim,* you will need to exercise your spiritual senses. Jesus operated under an open heaven throughout His ministry. The heavens opened over Him on the day He was baptized. The apostle John also saw and experienced the open heavens over Jesus in a profound way on several occasions and then later interacted with an open heaven himself (see Luke 3:21; Matt. 17:1-13; Rev. 4:1; John 1:51).

By finding an open heaven, or creating an open heaven over your life, you can easily recognize the angels that are all around you. (The dynamics of the phenomenon called an open heaven is addressed in great detail in the second book of this trilogy.)

Once the Lord opened my spiritual eyes in Canada and I saw angels, I purposed in my heart to storm the gates of Heaven until they opened over my life. You can storm the heavens too. Today there are still places in southwest Virginia where angelic activity is ongoing because of people's prayers, fasting, and decrees of God's Word that ripped open the heavens there. I have on numerous occasions seen hundreds of angels waving at me as I drive along a section of route 460 near Bluefield, Virginia. The heavens are still open there, and the angels are still active in that place. Moravian Falls, North Carolina, is another such place. Many people encounter angels in Moravian Falls. My 12-year-old daughter Miranda has seen angels as we have walked through the area. Find an open heaven, and you will find angelic activity. Spiritual maturity is not always necessary.

Exercising Your Spiritual Senses

Another important thing that we can do is to massage our spiritual gift or ability to see or perceive angels according to the principle of Hebrews 5:14. Once we begin to entertain angels and perceive that they are present, we are ready to begin to ask the Lord for His guidance and direction from the Holy Spirit to direct our steps (see John 14:26). We can massage our spiritual giftings and build them up in the same way that a weight lifter builds his muscles in the natural. We also have the invitation in the Scriptures to earnestly desire spiritual gifts. Look at First Corinthians 12:31: *"Earnestly desire the best gifts...."* We can ask the Lord according to the principle of Matthew 7:7 to give us a greater measure of gifting and to activate our gift of discerning of spirits. This of course will allow us to see into the realm of the spirit and discern angels.

Learning to Work in Symphony With the Holy Spirit

As we grow in the knowledge of how Christ's Kingdom operates, we will begin to recognize when the Holy Spirit is hovering around us. When we begin to minister in symphony with the authority and direction of the Holy Spirit, we may be instructed to release or employ angels to touch the realm of the earth. Remember the testimony I shared about the angel that manifested in Peru and healed the elderly woman's vision? This occurred because I was able to hear the Lord clearly and was obedient to act as I was instructed. We should listen carefully to the Holy Spirit and be obedient to do the things that He shows us to do, including loosing angelic ministry. This involves a bit of a learning curve, and it may take times of practice and waiting upon the Lord to perfect this ability to work in symphony with the Holy Spirit to activate angelic ministry (see John 16:13). It is important to be patient and practice persistence.

EVANGELISM AND WORSHIP OF JESUS

Other keys to help you understand how to interact with angels are often found during evangelism and worship of Jesus. The times that I have experienced the most angelic activity was in circumstances when I was worshiping Jesus with all of my heart. Anytime you are involved with worship of your King, you are in a position to recognize and experience angelic ministry. Sometimes you just need to ask the Lord to activate your spiritual senses to recognize the angels that are involved in the worship.

We have also experienced increased angelic activity in places where the everlasting Gospel of Jesus Christ is being preached. We are living in a day when the Lord will dramatically increase angels with the assignment and anointing of taking the Gospel to other places. Harvest angels will manifest to evangelists and give them supernatural direction and revelation as to when and where to minister. As you are involved in evangelism, you can expect to benefit from angelic visitations and ministry (see Acts 8:26-27; Rev. 14:6).

As we grow and mature in our spiritual gifting of discerning of spirits, we will begin to recognize that angels are around us at all times. I have also perceived angels in small groups as we speak about Jesus and His marvelous deeds. At other times as Kathy and I are sitting quietly speaking of the Lord, we will feel the "winds of heaven" stir around us. We both instantly understand that a scribe angel has manifested to record our words and the intents of our hearts. We will investigate the "books of Heaven" and the scribe angels that are assigned to record them. When believers gather and speak about the Lord, scribe angels are often present to record the words and works. Remember to entertain them (see Mal. 3:16).

We have reviewed several keys and spiritual tools that will help you develop your ability to encounter the angels in your life. Everyone has at least one angel assigned to them. However, there are many others ways that God can open your spiritual eyes that we have not considered in this chapter. Indeed, this is a very short list of the methods that can activate angelic help in your life. For example, we have not touched on God's sovereignty. God is the Lord of the universe, and He can do whatever He wishes, such as sending an angel to your house (see Ps. 115:3; 135:6).

As you have read the biblical and modern-day testimonies of angelic ministry, you will have found these keys evident in them all. In most of our testimonies, these keys are present in a combination of two or more, or in various combinations and formulas. You can believe that the Lord will also show you what the right combination for you is. Be open to God's leadings.

I have heard it said that "we are way too comfortable with a God that we barely know." That is a very true statement. We have no idea of the vastness, goodness, mercy, and love of our wonderful Father. The Lord has good things in store for us. Our heavenly Father gives good gifts to His children who wait upon Him and seek His Kingdom (see Ps. 100:5; Lam. 3:25).

DRAW CLOSE TO JESUS

When we seek God and His Kingdom and draw close to Him, He has promised to draw close to us. James 4:8 gives us this promise: *"Draw near to God and He will draw near to you…."* Consider practicing this list of spiritual exercises and these eight basic keys that can help activate angelic ministry in your life. You may also wish to violently storm the gates of Heaven with your prayers. The Lord can reveal even more reasons that can help you build your faith for God to open the angelic realms to you as you seek His Kingdom with your whole heart.

Finally, we must remember that Jesus the Lord has given us an example to follow. The Lord told us, *"I have given you an example, that you should do as I have done…"* (John 13:15). Jesus encourages us to do the things that He has done. We have learned that Jesus experienced the benefits of angelic ministry. Jesus prophesied about angelic ministry; He even promised that He would employ angelic ministry upon the earth in the coming days. That means that we can do those same things. We have a standing invitation to pray and *ask* our Father for the release of angels to help us in our times of need today (see Matt. 26:53).

In the next two chapters, we will look at the scriptural "nuts and bolts" that allow us to see and work with angels. Being aware of these simple scriptural principles will empower you to exercise your spiritual senses and grow in faith, gifting, and authority to demonstrate Christ's Kingdom.

Chapter 14

ANGELS AND THE GIFT OF DISCERNING OF SPIRITS

It is important to understand how the Lord opens our eyes to see angels. Let's look at some scriptural principles that will help familiarize us with the process of how the Lord activates our ability to see and work with the Lord's angels. Let's start by seeking to comprehend how it is possible for us to perceive angels which inhabit another realm or dimension. Some people call this *discernment*. That is true, but the ability to perceive angelic beings is actually a gift given to people by the Holy Spirit.

I would like to take some time to elaborate on the gifts of the Spirit—the Holy Spirit—particularly the gift of discerning of spirits (see 1 Cor. 12:4-12,13). First Corinthians 12:10 says, *"To another* [person is given] *the working of miracles, to another prophecy, to another discerning of spirits...."* It is the Holy Spirit who gives to people the spiritual gift of *"discerning of spirits."* The word used in this passage of Scripture for "spirits" is the Greek word *pneuma*. *Pneuma* is defined in Strong's Concordance as a current of air, breath, the spirit of God, Christ's Spirit or the Holy Spirit, a spirit, or an angel or demon.[1]

Pneuma is also the same word used for ministering spirits in Hebrews 1:13-14: *"But to which of the angels has He ever said: ...Are they not all ministering spirits sent forth to minister for those who will inherit salvation?"* Clearly this Greek word *pneuma* can refer to angels. It is clear that the gift of *discerning of spirits* can refer to the ability or gift to comprehend the presence of angelic beings.

It is also important to note that the gift of discerning of spirits is associated with the "power gifts" of healings, miracles, and prophecy. These gifts at times work in tandem and unity with each other. The spiritual gift of discerning of spirits is the ability to discern or recognize beings, good or evil, from the spiritual realm. When your spiritual eyes are activated and you begin to operate in the gift of discerning of spirits, you will see both the angelic realm and the demonic realm. A very important reason that the power gifts of miracles and healings operate in tandem with the gift of discerning of spirits is that often you are allowed to see demons that are associated with sickness and disease. When you see these spirits of infirmity, you have the authority to cast them out and thereby release healing or deliverance to the person who is oppressed by such a demon.

On numerous occasions, we have seen these spirits of infirmity. I have seen one spirit of infirmity that is associated with the flu. It looks like a combination of a Chihuahua dog, a bat, and a monkey. I have seen this spirit of infirmity clinging onto many sick people. When I command the devil to loose the person in the name of Jesus, the demon jumps off the person's back and scampers away, whimpering as it goes. Other spirits of infirmity look like various types of serpents. These can be associated with chronic headaches, breathing problems, body pain, and especially back problems. Again, when you see these spirits of infirmity, you have all authority over them. The Lord first began to show these things to me in 2001 to equip me to release healing to His people in Africa.

There are other types of demonic devices that you will be able to perceive when the gift of discerning of spirits is activated in your life.

At times, you will see the enemy's weapons of war. I have on many occasions seen arrows, chains, knives, shackles, or darts that have pierced people suffering from a number of debilitating conditions. When you remove the demonic weapons, these people are almost always immediately made whole.

It is important that we also employ our weapons of warfare (see Eph. 6:12; 2 Cor. 10:4). One powerfully sharp sword of the spirit is Isaiah 54:17:

> *'No weapon formed against you shall prosper, and every tongue which rises against you in judgment you shall condemn. This is the heritage of the servants of the Lord, and their righteousness is from Me,' says the Lord* (Isaiah 54:17).

God has given us the power and authority to condemn every word curse that is spoken against us and bind every demonic assignment that is associated with those curses. There is no need to be concerned when you begin to perceive evil things. You have all authority over them.

ANGELS MANIFEST TO OUR CARNAL SENSES

You have seen from the testimonies that it is possible to discern angels with all five of your carnal senses: sight, hearing, touch, smell, and taste. You have read modern-day examples of angelic ministry that have manifested to all of these senses. Remember that learning to perceive angelic activity can be a process. The Holy Spirit is assigned to guide and teach you all things. This is especially true concerning spiritual truths and phenomenon. (See John 14:26.) Since the Holy Spirit imparts the gift of discerning of spirits, He can also guide you and teach you all things concerning this spiritual gift.

We need only to ask Him for the wisdom we need (see Col. 1:9-10; James 1:5). Scripture clearly illustrates this concept. We have an open invitation to ask the Lord to give us spiritual understanding. This refers to comprehending the attributes of the realm of the spirit. We also have a wonderful invitation to seek God for help, understanding, and spiritual wisdom.

You will recall that at times I experienced the angelic realm as I perceived angels with all five of my physical senses. By entertaining the angels that I perceived, I exercised my spiritual senses by reason of use. When I began to massage my spiritual senses, the Spirit of God helped me understand principles concerning angels. The amount of angelic activity in my life greatly increased over a period of several years during this process of exercising my spiritual senses. You can also entertain angels and exercise your spiritual senses the same way.

Look at Hebrews 5:14: *"Solid food* [hidden or mysterious principles, or weightier matters of God's Kingdom] *belongs to those who are of full age, that is, those who by reason of use have their senses exercised to discern both good and evil."* We can grow and mature our spiritual senses in the same way that a weight lifter builds his biceps as we seek to comprehend the spiritual elements of the Kingdom of God.

Activating the gift of discerning of spirits in your life can be as simple as taking a step of faith and asking the Lord for it. Many people have shared with me that they see "flashes" or "streams of light" and have thought they were encountering angels. Many times when you "get a feeling" that angels are present, they are. You need to massage your spiritual senses to step into the realm of the Spirit. If you are seeing "flashes" or "streams of light," a simple prayer can help activate your gift of discerning of spirits. Ask. Activating your ability to discern or perceive angelic activity can be that simple (see Matt. 7:7).

It does not matter which of your five senses that you perceive angels with; they are all valid. You can be released or activated into the gift of discerning of spirits through any one of your five senses—by the sense of sight, hearing, touch, smell, or taste. You have seen in the testimonies that angels have been revealed to people through all of these physical senses. It is also important to remember that you can also encounter angels in your dreams. There are hundreds of ways that the Lord can open up the heavens to you and allow you to interact with angels. You need not be concerned, focused, or fixated on any one method.

OUR SPIRITUAL SENSES

The apostle Paul prays an "apostolic prayer" in Ephesians 1:16-23. Paul prays that *"the eyes of your understanding"* be enlightened. We all have a "knowing" released to us by the Holy Spirit. This supernatural knowledge can be also defined as the gift of discerning of spirits working in symphony with the unction of the Holy Spirit. When Paul prays for *"the eyes of your understanding,"* he is not referring to our natural eyesight. Paul is referring to the eyes of the soul or spirit, our supernatural vision. Paul prays for our spiritual ability to perceive phenomenon from the spiritual realm to increase. The word here for *understanding* can mean deep thought or supernatural thought or mind. It can also mean to have the mind of God, the mind of the Spirit of God, or to have or experience the mind of Christ. Paul desired people to understand that they have a spiritual inheritance and spiritual nature that they can step into.

We need to understand our true nature in Christ. We have the mind of Christ. When the eyes of our understanding are opened, we begin to appreciate who we really are "in Christ Jesus;" we begin to see and enter into the Kingdom of Heaven. And when we enter into the realms of Heaven, we can begin to appropriate the power and authority that are our heavenly inheritance. Our spiritual senses allow us to be transformed into the likeness of Christ Jesus—and activated into the reality of angelic ministry, just like Jesus.

Our spiritual senses also enable us to step into the spirit or heavenly places where our supernatural inheritance is waiting for us. Spiritual senses are an element of our very being. We are creatures created by God in His image with a spirit, soul, and body. Our five physical senses are the operation of our body, or carnal self. The eyes of our understanding, or our spiritual senses, operate in the spiritual realm the way our five carnal senses detect elements in the natural realm. Our spiritual senses perceive elements and phenomena from the spirit.

When the eyes of our understanding are activated, we begin to experience life through our spirit, and that part of our being becomes dominant in terms of perception. This can last for a few seconds, or it can last for days as we learn how to walk in the spirit. In Enoch's life, this was eternal (see Gen. 5:24). That is what I want! This can be the outworking of the gift of discerning of spirits activating in your life. Spiritual understanding can also be the gifts of prophecy, word of knowledge, and word of wisdom manifesting in your life.

The Holy Spirit plays an important role in the implementation and release of His spiritual gifts, and spiritual understanding. Some people call this revelation, or the spirit of wisdom and understanding or revelation. (See Isaiah 11:2.) At times the Holy Spirit in us can alert us to supernatural or angelic activity. Of course the opposite is also true. The Holy Spirit can also activate our spiritual senses and alert us to the presence and activity of the demonic realm, or demonic spirits.

We could define this operation of our spiritual senses like this. Our spiritual senses are, on occasion, an extension of the gift of discerning of spirits, and the other revelatory gifts mentioned previously (the gift of prophecy, word of knowledge, and word of wisdom). Our spiritual senses at times will work in symphony with the Holy Spirit that dwells within us. Understanding this dynamic of how the Holy Spirit acti-vates our spiritual senses can be a process. It can take time to understand how to work in symphony with the precious Holy Spirit to recognize and release or work with His gifts. This understanding will ultimately enable us to activate or "loose" God's angels as we learn and understand how to co-labor with them. As we have stated, this can be a learning curve. However, we can press into the kingdom of God and ask the Lord for wisdom and revelation in this area.

One scriptural tool that we can employ to accelerate this process is Paul's apostolic prayer. The apostle Paul prays for the activation of the eyes of our hearts. Paul is seeking to increase our ability to perceive the supernatural and angelic activity that is all around us. I suggest that you consider praying Paul's prayer over your life on a daily basis (see Eph. 1:16-23). This will help you to activate your spiritual senses. It is also possible to pray in the spirit with understanding, asking for the "eyes of your understanding" to be enlightened. This can help us to receive the revelation of our riches of glory of God's spiritual inheritance within each of us. An important aspect of this spiritual inheritance is the unction and giftings of the Holy Spirit. Remember Paul encouraged people to walk in the spirit (see Gal. 5:16,25).

Understanding how our spiritual senses operate in relation-ship to the supernatural should not be considered a "fearful" idea or proposition. God is a Spirit. He dwells in a spiritual Kingdom. If you hope to enter into Heaven, you are striving to enter God's supernatural and spiritual home. The reality is that the spiritual Kingdom of Heaven is all around you at this second. The realm of the Spirit where Jesus Christ is seated at the right hand of the Father is more real than the book that you are holding in your hands. The ability to enter into this spiritual Kingdom and realm of the Spirit should be normal for us. However, we have allowed the world to steal our spiritual heritage, the supernatural, which has now become paranormal to most people. The opposite should be true. We should be at home in the supernatural realm where our God dwells. You should not be paranoid of the paranormal.

Jesus put it this way:

> *The hour is coming, and now is, when the true worshipers will worship the Father in spirit and truth; for the Father is seeking such to worship Him. God is Spirit, and those who worship Him must worship in spirit and truth* (John 4:23-24).

The word translated as *spirit* in this passage is also the Greek word *pneuma*. The Lord actually uses language that indicates He wants us to kiss Him and worship Him in the spiritual realm.[2] We are actually welcome and have standing invitations to access the spiritual realm where angels dwell. We can enter that place without "trespassing" because of the finished work of Calvary and the precious blood of the Lamb of God. The Cross of Calvary is the most important key and only bridge to legitimate angelic encounters. (See Colossians 3:1 and Ephesians 2:6.)

We all have a spiritual inheritance and nature that we can step into. The Lord will accelerate this process in the coming season. Multitudes of people will access the Kingdom of

Heaven and start to exercise their spiritual senses by reason of use in the approaching season. They will surely begin to experience the supernatural elements of God's Kingdom. Occasionally, this will include encounters with angels. As angelic encounters become more common in your life, you will begin to overcome the fear of the unknown. You will have supernatural encounters, and you will need to understand how to evaluate such experiences properly. Several practical and helpful principles concerning understanding angelic encounters are discussed in the next chapter.

ENDNOTES

1. "Pneuma"; see http://www.studylight.org/lex/grk/view .cgi?number=4151.

2. See http://strongsnumbers.com/greek/4352.htm.

Chapter 15

EVALUATING YOUR
ANGELIC ENCOUNTERS

There are three basic principles you should consider when evaluating any supernatural experience. This holds true whether you are considering prophecy, prophetic experiences, dreams, trances, visions, and, of course, angelic encounters. These three principles are *revelation*, *interpretation*, and *implementation*. For the sake of this book, we will look at these principles in relationship to angelic ministry and encounters. However, you can apply these principles to any spiritual experience.

REVELATION

It is absolutely necessary that we practice sound biblical principles when experiencing angelic ministry or seeking to activate angelic ministry in our lives. Any revelation that we receive as a result of angelic encounters must agree and line up with Scripture. The Holy Spirit will not contradict Himself. The canon of Scripture was written by the Spirit of God as the Lord spoke through holy men and friends of God. Moses was one of these holy men (see Exod. 33:11; 2 Pet. 1:20-21).

Any revelation that is contrary to the Word of God and principles set forth therein must be immediately disregarded. For our purposes, we can define *revelation* as "any knowledge, information, or facts that are obtained from an angelic encounter." These revelations can take the form of spoken or perceived words, audible words, Scripture, visions, and dreams.

Edification and Exhortation

Any angelic encounter that emanates from the Lord should bring a revelation that edifies. However, sometimes angelic visitations can also bring into our hearts a holy fear. True angelic encounters are often accompanied with a fearful response. This is a common human reaction to the manifestation of an angel. (See Daniel 10:12; Matthew 28:5; Luke 1:13,30; 2:10.)

A fearful response is a useful barometer to measure angelic encounters. It is normal to experience great fear or terror in the presence of God's holy angels. As you press in and begin to operate in the gift of discerning of spirits, you will find that angelic encounters are not always fearful. Some angelic encounters can seem normal, but others may scare the wits out of you. However, any true heavenly angelic encounter should bring conviction and not condemnation. *Conviction* is the sovereign work of the Holy Spirit. *Condemnation* is the work of the enemy of our soul (see Rom. 8:1). We need to understand the difference between the Holy Spirit's conviction and the enemy's condemnation.

Here is an important strategy to help you understand supernatural revelation. A true angelic encounter should bring good fruit or the fruit of the Spirit and edification. If your angelic encounter leads you to one of the fruits of the Spirit such as love, joy, peace, longsuffering, kindness, goodness, faithfulness, gentleness, or self-control, then you can proceed to consider this angelic encounter further by bathing it in prayer, and if necessary, fasting. However, if your angelic encounter or supernatural revelation leads to the works of the flesh: adultery, fornication, uncleanness, lewdness, idolatry, sorcery, hatred, contentions, jealousies, outbursts of wrath, selfish ambitions, dissensions, heresies, envy, murders, drunkenness, revelries, etc., then the visitation or revelation should be disregarded (see Gal. 5:20-23). If an angel or any other supernatural revelation leads you to act contrary to the principles in Scripture, you should dismiss the encounter and associated revelation (see Gal. 1:8-9).

Test the Spirits

Legitimate angelic encounters will exalt Jesus Christ. Any angelic encounter that results in revelation that does not exalt Christ Jesus as the Son of God should be immediately dismissed.

First John 4:1-3 encourages us to *"test the spirits."* This is a great passage of Scripture to implement when testing angelic encounters.

> *Do not believe every spirit, but **test the spirits**,*
> *whether they are of God....By this you know*
> *the Spirit of God: Every spirit that confesses*
> *that Jesus Christ has come in the flesh is of*
> *God, and every spirit that does not confess that*
> *Jesus Christ has come in the flesh is not of God.*
> *And this is the spirit of the Antichrist...* (John
> 4:1-3).

The word used for *spirit* here is the Greek word *pneuma* meaning an angel or demon. Clearly, not all spiritual beings exalt Jesus Christ. Test the spirits.

Demonic beings cannot speak about the blood of Jesus; neither can they exalt Christ's finished work of the Cross or His deity. You have the authority to test the spirits by asking them to confess Jesus Christ as Lord: *"Every spirit that does not confess that Jesus Christ has come in the flesh is not of God. And this is the spirit of the Antichrist* [or devil]" (1 John 4:3). This is a God-given tool that you can employ to test the spirits and to protect yourself from deception when encountering any spiritual being.

Friendship With Jesus

It is also imperative that we are in right relationship with the Lord before we seek to utilize angelic ministry or access the realms of the heavens. Jesus promised each of us that we have the God-given right and ability to become God's friend. This is a gift of grace and not works. We can realize His friendship. This often comes by the simple revelation that we can have friendship with the Lord. As we come to this understanding, the Lord will begin to share heavenly revelations and hidden treasures with us because we are in relationship and friendship with Him. The Lord encourages His friends to search out the hidden treasure of the realms of Heaven (see Matt. 13:44; Ps. 25:14). The Lord has called us His family (see Gal. 3:26). As joint heirs with Christ, we also have access to all of the heavenly treasures Jesus has at His disposal in the heavenly places. One of the liberties or supernatural rights that Jesus has is the ability to perceive angels and the authority to release angelic ministry. We have that privilege and equivalent authority because of our lineage and relationship with God. If you are in right relationship with God then you already have this privilege and authority.

Disclosure and Accountability

Finally, you should disclose any revelation that comes from an angelic encounter with your pastoral or apostolic overseer. If you are hesitant to share any angelic encounter with spiritual authority, then this should be a warning signal that something may be amiss. We firmly believe in accountability and submission to the local church and leadership therein.

Your overseer should be someone with whom you have the liberty to disclose all of your angelic experiences and supernatural encounters. This should be your first priority if you are not involved in a local church. Please find a Spirit-led ministry and seek their wisdom, guidance, and support. If you have any questions concerning any angelic encounters, you should disclose these to your pastors or apostolic authority. If they recommend a course of action, then you should be submissive and obedient to their suggestions and advice. Disclosure, submission, and accountability are critical to ensure that you are protected from the possibility of deception. Please seek to follow these biblical principles as you begin to experience angelic encounters. Once your angelic encounter has passed all of these tests, then you may wish to proceed to the next step and seek the Lord for an interpretation of your experience.

INTERPRETATION

Consider all angelic visitations carefully. It is a good idea to write down angelic encounters as soon as possible. This way, you can document the ongoing unfolding of the experience. You might be surprised to learn that most people have a tendency to forget details about angelic encounters. By keeping them in a journal, you can revisit the facts at a later time.

Here are a few things to consider about angelic encounters and any revelation that is obtained from the supernatural. Ask yourself this question: "Did this encounter have a witness with my spirit?" The Holy Spirit resides within you as a believer in Christ Jesus. As such, the Holy Spirit will have a "witness" with godly, angelic encounters (see 1 John 5:7). At times, you will have a "knowing" that an encounter was of God, and there will be no question about it. Your spirit will bear witness with the Holy Spirit.

Unction From the Holy One

At other times, you will have a "check in your spirit." When this happens, you will find that you are unsettled or ill at ease with an experience. If these emotions are present, then you should seriously question the validity of an angelic encounter. Another spiritual principle that can help you develop this attribute is found in First John 2:20: *"But ye have an unction from the Holy One, and ye know all things"* (KJV). The unction of the Holy Ghost can help you have a sovereign knowing of all things.

Praying in the Spirit

Praying in the Spirit can help activate your spirit to begin to perceive, hear, sense, and then to see into the realm of the Spirit. (See Jude 20.) Praying in the Spirit activated the eyes of my heart, and I was launched into the gifting to see angels. If you purpose in your heart to pray in tongues for extended periods of time, you will be activated in a similar manner. I challenge you to invest 24 hours praying in the Holy Spirit nonstop. I guarantee that something will break open over your life. It is possible that it may be the gift of discerning of spirits. Your spiritual senses will come alive. If you do not pray in tongues, you can still intercede in your own style of prayer. Praying in the spirit can help to give you a supernatural understanding of angelic encounters.

Prayer, Fasting, and Waiting on the Lord

At times, angelic experiences will be very clear in the revelation that you are given as a result of an angelic visitation. The intended meaning will be very clear to you. However, at other times, angelic encounters will not leave you with a clear interpretation or meaning. You may have a witness in your spirit that what you experienced was of God, but you may not be sure what it means to you. This can be the case with angelic visitations that occur in visions or dreams. When this occurs, it is important to wait upon the Lord in a posture of meditative prayer and seeking. Remember that Daniel had to wait 21 days for the answer to his prayer and the interpretation that he was seeking from the Lord. The combination of prayer with fasting is critical to the interpretation of some angelic encounters. (See Daniel 10:13; Psalm 119:15; Philippians 4:8.)

Confirmation of Supernatural Encounters

The Lord is always kind and considerate to our need to understand supernatural events and gives us the confirmation of supernatural occurrences in our lives. Confirmation can come in many forms. At times, it takes the form of a Scripture. Remember the testimony that I shared in Chapter 5 about the encounter that I had in Tanzania with the angelic hosts and the visitation of Jesus? The Holy Spirit led me to a Scripture that confirmed that angelic encounter for me (see John 1:51).

God may also release confirmation to you in a number of other ways. When I experienced a visitation of the Holy Spirit in Newfoundland, the Lord arranged for me to take the book *Good Morning, Holy Spirit* by Benny Hinn with me into the wilderness. Benny's book was an instant confirmation to my supernatural experience. You will usually recognize God's confirmation because you will have a great witness in your spirit that God has spoken to you to confirm an experience orchestrated by Him.

You need to ask the Lord for wisdom regarding what steps you should take to implement the interpretation of the revelation you have received from the supernatural experience. Write down a step-by-step plan and discuss your plan of action with your apostolic or pastoral authority before taking any action. Once you have firmed up the interpretation of your experience, it is wise to allow plenty of time when walking out these steps. There is no need to rush to a quick decision or course of action. It is best to bathe all such revelation in a great deal of prayer. Timing is vital. It is also important to seek the counsel of as many trusted friends and spiritual leaders as possible (see Prov. 11:14). It is best to be cautious, patient, and sure when evaluating angelic encounters. Once you are sure of the interpretation of the supernatural knowledge, (revelation), that you are given from your angelic encounter, then you can consider taking action.

IMPLEMENTATION

You will recall the testimony that I shared about encountering Jesus and four angels at Murchison Falls, Uganda. In that angelic encounter I heard very clearly from the Lord. I was given the revelation and direction to move to another city and to submit to the pastor of a specific church. That angelic encounter was life-changing. From the very beginning, I had a total peace, or witness, in my spirit about the experience.

Nonetheless, I did fast and pray about this experience. I also studied the Scriptures to see if there were any examples of angelic ministry like this in the Bible. Would angels be involved in directing a person to move from one city to another city or geographical location? I found in Acts 16:9-10 one such example in the ministry of Paul. Paul received instruction to travel to another city. I also found in the Scriptures where an angel led Philip to another geographic area (see Acts 8:26).

Not only did my experiences line up with the Scriptures, but I had a great inner witness that this was of the Lord. However, I also submitted this angelic encounter to my pastor at that time, Omega Dowell. I asked for her wisdom and insight. She prayed about this for me. Later she told me that she felt that it was "of God." Momma Dowell encouraged me to wait for God's perfect timing for this to manifest. I listened to the advice that I was given by my spiritual overseer. Indeed, it took another three years for the move to take place. By that time, the Lord had orchestrated every possible aspect of the move to Kansas City.

I encourage you to follow this process and submit to each step of this method—revelation, interpretation, and implementation. There are several questions that you need to ask yourself about the encounter (revelation), the interpretation (what you discern, learn, or understand from the angelic encounter), and the implementation (what course of action you take as a result of what you've learned).

REVELATION FOR INTERCESSION

We are coming into a time when the Lord will begin to release angelic ministry to us for intercession. Many of us in the Body of Christ will begin to have supernatural experiences where we will be "caught up" into the realms of Heaven and have angelic encounters. Often, we will be allowed to obtain supernatural revelation from the realms of Heaven as a result of angelic ministry. I have found that many times the revelation that we receive from angelic encounters is never meant to be shared. Often, the revelation is released to us for prayer and intercession only. We are not supposed to divulge it to anyone but God as we pray it back to Him. I call this "third-heaven intercession." (We will look at this aspect of angelic ministry in much more detail in the second and third books of this trilogy. This is a very important aspect of the imminent release of angelic ministry today.) As we enter into this season, many people will experience angelic phenomenon on a regular basis. It is important that we understand how to co-labor with God's messengers. Many times we will work with God's angels in prayer. We will need to work in concert with angels and the divine revelation that they share with us as they visit the earth, or as we are allowed to visit them in the heavens. Godly angels are our fellow servants of Christ Jesus. We should welcome the angels that are already busy working around each of us now.

By this three-step process, you can glean heavenly direction and comprehend how to release what you know upon the earth. You can at times work with angels to move the things that are in the spirit or the realms of the heavens to earth. We can implement Jesus' guidelines for prayer in Luke 11:2: *"...When you pray, say: ...Your kingdom come. Your will be done on earth as it is in heaven."* It is true. Angels are still sent from Heaven in answer to our prayers, to release favor, revelation, healings, miracles, and spiritual experiences in our lives today. However, we must remember to consider all angelic encounters through the lens of Scripture. Let's investigate more modern-day testimonies about how angels touch people's lives. In the next chapter, we will investigate "guardian angels," or angels of protection.

Chapter 16

GUARDIAN ANGELS

One of the most popular beliefs in modern culture is that people have "guardian angels." In fact, that is very true. One of the main duties of angels is to protect people. In Psalm 91, we see that God gives His angels charge over us. The implication of the word *charge* here is "to make responsible for, give charge over, or to empower with responsibility or duty, and authority for one's care, or custody." (See Strongs Concordance Reference #H6680.) Psalm 91:11 states, *"For He shall give His angels charge over you, to keep you in all your ways."* Another clear example of this type of angelic protection is found in Psalm 34:7: *"The angel of the Lord encamps all around those who fear Him, and delivers them."* Both of these Scriptures speak of guardian angels.

This type of angelic ministry will also increase in the coming days as the world grows darker and more dangerous.

We have many testimonies of this kind but cannot write about them all. However, let's look at a few dramatic examples.

ANGELS FOR PROTECTION

In 2006, I experienced a powerful angelic visitation that is a great example of how God can use an angel to give direction for protection. Bishop Zenobius Isaya was in the room during this angelic encounter. We were staying in the Imperial Botanical Beach Hotel, room 25, in Kampala, on our way to Northern Uganda to learn more about building orphanages and helping orphans. Our trip to Gulu was coincidentally timed to fall within a short-lived cease-fire between the Ugandan Army and the LRA (Lord's Resistance Army, militant rebels). Isaya and I had enjoyed a good dinner and were settling into our room. We were uneasy about traveling into a war zone. Around 10 P.M., we both fell into an uneasy sleep after we had prayed together asking the Lord for protection, wisdom, and direction for the trip. About 2 A.M., I sat up in the bed, and the fear of the Lord was hanging thickly in the room. There was also a bright light that was hurting my eyes.

I looked up into the corner of the room and saw a large ball of lightning hovering. The ball of light was about 18 inches in circumference, and it hovered about 10 feet in the air. Every hair on my body stood on end, and the fear of God flooded my spirit. I had a strong desire to crawl under the carpet or floor if possible. I rolled off the bed and fell prostrate upon the floor. Bishop Isaya had already hit the floor.

From time to time, I peeked open my eyes. The light seemed to grow brighter. As the light of the visitor grew brighter, it seemed that the glory of God also increased in our room. Finally, I realized that the Lord was trying to do something and asked, "Lord, what are you trying to do here tonight?"

Instantly, I had revelation. Words filled my mind. "You must be careful when you travel to Gulu. There will be great danger there." The angel went on, "You must fast and pray while you are in Gulu. No harm will befall you and your company. Do not fear; God's presence will go before you and give you rest."

I raised my head, and I saw the ball of light "shimmer out." The angel had been in the room for about 20 minutes. When I asked Isaya what he had experienced, he told me that he had "seen the angel of God."

I believe that the Lord sent this angelic messenger in response to our prayers and also to keep us from harm's way. We did in fact find ourselves in hostile situations while in Gulu and in Pabo at the Displaced People's Camp where we ministered in a small crusade. However, the memory of the angelic visitation gave us great faith and courage to preach in some very hostile environments. This was similar to the visitation that Paul experienced in Acts 27. It was a "rocky trip," but we were kept safe in the face of real danger and threats.

A GUARDIAN ANGEL SURPRISES MY NEW FRIEND

After returning from Malawi in 2003, I was given reassurance about the angel that seemed to be following me around. I was walking in a marvelous gift of faith when I returned to the United States. As I prayed about the outreach ministry that was planned for Las Vegas, the Lord gave me a vision. The Holy Spirit said, "You will meet a blind man in Las Vegas. You will know when you see him. He will be healed just like those you prayed for in Africa. He will be totally blind in one eye and have little vision in his other eye. He is expecting to be healed."

After the first session in Las Vegas, I went with a group of friends to lunch. As we were sitting at the table, the Lord spoke to me, "Go sit down at that table over there." I jumped up, went over to the table, and sat down with four strangers. After awhile, the man next to me began to shake all over and fell down on the floor vibrating! After that, the others at the table were interested in hearing about the miracles that had just happened in Malawi. I told them about Leonard growing a new eyeball, and the 72 blind who were healed with the help of the angel. I also told them about the healing angel. Chuck was very curious and had a lot of questions for me.

Later, I told them a blind man would be healed in Las Vegas. Amazingly, when we left the restaurant, the Holy Spirit spoke to me, saying, "Get ready, here comes the blind man you are supposed to pray for." As two of us were standing in front of the restaurant, an older black man was walking in our direction. I said, "Here comes the blind man; the Lord is going to heal him right now." The man was still about four feet away.

"Excuse me, can I pray for you? You are blind in one eye and can barely see out of the other. Jesus wants to heal you today."

A big smile spread slowly across the man's face. "The Lord told me that He was going to send someone and heal my eyes. I have been waiting for this a long time."

Suddenly, I felt the healing angel step up behind me. I prayed, and Jesus immediately healed his blind eye, and he began to laugh. He did a little jig. "Praise Jesus, I can see!" He shook my hand and walked away a little more quickly than he had approached. Later Chuck decided that he wanted to "hang out with me" and find out more about the "angels and stuff." However, during those first days in Las Vegas, I don't think he totally believed the testimonies I was sharing with him about angels, especially when I told him that Jesus had given me two angels and one was assigned to protect me. The other angel was assigned to help release healing as we co-labored together.

Houston, We Have Lift-Off

Before we left Las Vegas, we decided to ride the Slingshot together. The Slingshot is an action ride mounted on top of Circus Circus Casino. When the Slingshot blasted us into the air, I hung suspended in the air for a fraction of a second weightless. At that precise moment, the Lord spoke to me, "You have just been launched." The ride turned out to be a prophetic act; the Lord was referring to me being launched into full-time ministry.

Chuck had an interesting angelic encounter the night before we rode the Slingshot. He has a good sense of humor, and I think that he learned that the Lord also possesses a good sense of humor. Chuck was having a hard time getting his mind around some of the things I was telling him about angels being assigned to me in order to protect me from harm. We talked about angels quite a bit over those four days. The subject sort of became a running joke between us. Chuck would say things like, "Why don't you get your angel to pass me the salt?" and other things along those lines.

After a few days of good-natured ripping, I told Chuck that he should be careful or the Lord may have my angel take hold of him! That night as we were in the elevator at Circus Circus, my angel decided to introduce himself to Chuck. He had been kidding around on the ride to the top of the building, saying, "Well, you don't have to worry about getting on the ride with that angel of yours; he'll probably be on the ride with you!" The angel decided to turn the tables on my new friend.

When we arrived at the top floor at the entrance to the Slingshot, I stepped out of the elevator first. Suddenly, I heard a loud "ka-thump" in the elevator! I turned around and saw Chuck flattened against the back wall of the elevator. His eyes were as big as headlights! "What are you doing?" I asked. Chuck sort of shivered all over and stepped out of the elevator giving me a wide berth. It seemed that Chuck was shoved back into the elevator by a large, unseen hand! My guardian angel had thought to protect me, or perhaps he was just a little tired of Chuck's jokes and ribbing. Chuck no longer joked with me anymore about my angel. Here is his testimony:

> During the conference, a few of us went to a Casino for a lunch buffet during a break in the meetings. As we were sitting at our table

eating lunch, this guy walks up and sits down on a bench next to our table and starts telling us about the trip that he had just returned from. As he is giving testimony to all of the miracles he had seen in Malawi, including the restoration of a man's missing eyeball, one of the people in our group literally fell out of his chair onto the floor. That was the first time I saw Kevin Basconi.

Later that day, we were organized into teams to go out and do prophetic ministry. I signed up for the Street Ministry team. As my group was meeting to get organized before going out, Kevin walked into the room. As Kevin was leaving, I heard myself say out loud, "I have a meeting with him later." Everyone gave me a funny look. As I was leaving the building, I noticed Kevin in one of the rooms, so I went up to him and said something like, "You know when you came into our meeting earlier? I really felt like I was supposed to meet with you."

Kevin said, "So, you'd like me to pray for you?" I said OK, and he began to pray for me. Shortly after he began praying for me, I found myself on the floor. After Kevin prayed for me, I started to experience new things. I could feel a weighty presence of the Holy Spirit and felt "intoxicated" by God's presence most of the time. I had manifestations of taste, fragrance, and felt an intimacy with God that I had never had before; I began having "third heaven" experiences. Kevin and I became friends during this time, and we spent a lot of time together. One night we decided to ride the Slingshot. While we were in the elevator, I began teasing Kevin about something.

When the door opened to the elevator, everyone walked out. I was the last one. As I moved forward to leave the elevator, I felt a hand on my chest that pushed me back against the wall of the elevator. It wasn't a violent push, more of a playful push, but strong enough to knock me off balance and fall against the wall. It was like something you would expect a friend to do when you had been teasing them. There was absolutely no one else in the elevator with me at the time. Everyone else had already gotten out.

I believe that what I experienced that night was the hand of an angel. I can't explain it, but I experienced it. I felt the hand on my chest, just as if it were that of a physical being pushing me back into that elevator; it left a lasting impression on me, no pun intended.

—CHUCK LOOSLI, Wasilla, Alaska

I believe that I was still walking under an open heaven when I returned from Malawi. It is possible that since I had broken through into the realm of the spirit and was seeing and interacting with the angelic realm that the fragrance of Heaven became attached to me. I was aware of constant angelic activity around me after the trip. I believe that an angel did in fact show my new friend that he was there to protect me and proved that fact to Chuck.

Some people break through and walk under an open heaven, and enter into the anointing by proximity. A great biblical example of this is found in Matthew 17 when Jesus and three disciples were on the Mount of Transfiguration. The disciples had the eyes of their understanding opened there, and the gift of discerning of spirits was activated in their lives because of their proximity to the open heaven that was over Jesus. (We will look at the reality of the open heavens that were upon and over Jesus in great detail in the second book of this trilogy.) Sometimes the anointing is better caught than taught (see Matt. 17:1-8; Mark 1:10). We continue looking at other duties of angels in the next chapter.

Chapter 17

OTHER IMPORTANT DUTIES OF ANGELS

I want to share a few more testimonies that illustrate the ways that you can expect to encounter angels. These testimonies will also help to outline several important obligations that angels fulfill in the lives of people. A common misconception is that all angelic experiences and encounters are "super-spiritual." Angelic visitations *can* be powerful, but at other times they can be quite normal as we grow and mature into this realm.

ANGELS ESCORT PEOPLE INTO HEAVEN

God dispatches angels to be present at the death of His people and carry their souls into Heaven. The Lord loves His people, and our deaths are important and even precious to Him (see Ps. 116:15). Jesus taught about this ministry of angels in Luke 16:22: *"So it was that the beggar died, and was carried by the angels to Abraham's bosom....*" The term Jesus used here, *Abraham's bosom,* refers to a location in Heaven, or paradise (see Matt. 8:11).

When my father, Miro, died on April 9, 1990, the glory and peace of Heaven immediately flooded his hospital room. The room was suddenly filled with the Lord's presence. My sister also reported that the anointing and peace of the Lord filled the room. My father smiled and entered into paradise consumed with the peace that surpasses all understanding. My sister's family was also given peace and reassurances that he did indeed pass into Heaven. I am convinced that angels were present to escort him into the presence of Jesus.

In August 2006, my mother Helen passed away. I was by her side for several days during this time. I stayed in the ICU with her most evenings between midnight and early morning. At times, Mom would rouse herself and speak to me. At those times, she was very lucid and made her wishes known to me. On the third night that I was with her, she rose up at about 2 A.M. to speak to me. She told me that she knew that she was going home to be with the Lord, and that I was not to worry because she had peace. Suddenly her eyes grew large, and she asked me, "Who are those two men by the door dressed in white?" I realized that Mom was seeing the angels sent on assignment to escort her into Heaven. Two nights later at about the same time, she sat up and said to me, "Look, honey, Jesus is here."

I had no remorse when Mom passed on, and have absolute certainty that she is now in her heavenly home with the Lord (see 2 Cor. 5:8). I also have complete assurance and peace that Mom was guided into the realms of paradise by the angels that she saw in her ICU room. Before she passed away, she gave me these instructions, "Stay close to Jesus, and keep preaching the Gospel." I think that is great advice for anyone reading this right now! Many people report encountering angels at the passing of loved ones, or when someone has a "near death" experience.

ANGELS IMPART DREAMS AND VISIONS

Many ordinary people are beginning to receive revelation when angels invade their dreams. I have been visited in a succession of dreams over the last few years and given a series of revelations. On several occasions, I have been visited by both the Lord Jesus and by angels in my dreams (see Job 33:15). This kind of angelic visitation should be seriously considered. An angelic encounter that occurs in a dream can be just as real as an open-eye encounter in the natural and should not be dismissed. God is still giving dreams and visions, as well as imparting the spirit of wisdom and understanding to interpret dreams, through angelic ministry today (see Gen. 28:11-17). We will also see that the Lord will begin to employ angelic dreams to speak clearly to us in this season. These angelic "God dreams" will give people direction and guidance.

We have stepped into a season when the Lord will begin to release dreams and visions in an accelerated manner. Many of these dreams will be released and birthed through angelic ministry. Joseph, the earthly father of Jesus, was visited by an angel in his dreams and given divine direction on numerous occasions (see Matt. 1:20; 2:13,19). God still uses angels to impart dreams to His children, and we will see this type of angelic ministry multiply in the coming days. Angels will be employed to "plant dreams" in ungodly rulers of the earth. This is what happened to Nebuchadnezzar in Daniel 4.

ANGELS WATCH AND RECORD THE AFFAIRS OF HUMANKIND

Angels record the activities of humankind. God at times calls for His heavenly books to be opened and reviews an individual's actions, words, or prayer requests. Cornelius is a good example of this. An angel appeared to him and told him that his alms had been brought up before the Lord (see Acts 10:3-4).

The Book of Malachi speaks of the book of remembrance. This is a book that is recorded in Heaven of an individual's doings. God assigns angels to scribe and record the lives, works, and words of men. Malachi 3:16 says, *"Then those who feared the Lord spoke to one another, and the Lord listened and heard them; so a book of remembrance was written before Him for those who fear the Lord and who meditate on His name."* Who else in Heaven could write in this book, save for His servants the angels? As mentioned previously, certain angels are anointed to write, and I call these angels scribe angels (see Ezekiel 9:1-4).

ANGELS AND SIGNS AND WONDERS

These kinds of angels are being released into every area of the earth at this hour. Angels that can impact the meteorological environment of a region are what I call "signs and wonders angels." When these angels appear, the atmosphere of the earthly realm is shaken, and supernatural signs appear in the heavens. This sometimes takes the form of an immediate change in the current weather pattern. Unusual meteorological phenomena can happen instantly or can crop up within minutes when these angels manifest or visit. We have seen portals appear in the heavens in Tanzania and Uganda during crusade meetings in association with "signs and wonders angels." It is customary to see "double rainbows" appear over the altar as we release the invitation for salvation. Double rainbows occurred on nine separate occasions, in nine different cities, during crusade meetings in 2007 alone.

Some individuals have suggested that angels are all the same size and appearance. However, I beg to differ. We have seen angels in a multitude of sizes and shapes. Not all assume the form of a human. We have witnessed angels that appeared as balls of light or lightning, wind, fire, and even whirlwinds of flames and phosphorescent colors.

We have seen one particularly large angel as we have preached crusades. This giant angel is at least 100 to 120 feet tall. He is of a fierce countenance. He has long, golden-blond hair streaming over his massive shoulders. He is always carrying a large shiny shield and a massive two-edged sword. He is usually preceded by smaller warrior angels. But when this large one appears, there is a breaking open of the heavenly realms.

I believe that this angel carries a powerful "breaker anointing" into specific geographic regions. I have seen and discerned this specific angel a handful of times as I have preached in crusades in Africa. I discerned him in Mwanza when a portal opened over the altar and the glory of God fell upon the crusade grounds resulting in hundreds of salvations. I believe that this kind of angel is similar to the ones that Jesus will release in the last days to reap the great harvest and to help people preach the Gospel. (We will look at the role of the Holy Spirit and signs and wonders angels in great detail in the second book of this trilogy.)

BUKOBA, TANZANIA

Let's look at a testimony from an individual who saw the "signs and wonders angel" in Bukoba, Tanzania. This angel is an example of huge angels that populate the realms of Heaven. When this angel shows up, there are often signs and wonders in the heavens above as he "touches down" (see Joel 2:30). This resulted in the "breaking open" of the heavens over the meetings and the release of notable miracles. These both help to ensure that salvation is multiplied (see Rev. 14:15). Here is Robyn Tan's testimony.

> I wanted to get the facts right about the angel that I saw in Tanzania, so I found my journal about the mission trip to Bukoba. That really helped to jog my memory, (although I did still remember the event). I saw the angel the first night of the crusade, August 24, 2005. There was a crowd of approximately 2,500 on the crusade grounds. Kevin had preached a great message, and then he called for women who had tumors to come forward to the altar.

It was then I saw in the spirit a very large angel who was standing at the back of the crowd. The angel's large wings spanned out right over the back of the crowd, and then the angel swept its wings over the crowd; simultaneously, as it did so, a group of women moved forward out of the crowd to be prayed for. It was quite amazing to see something in the spirit and something in the natural happen at the same time. This angel repeated this action a couple of times, and the same thing happened each time.

In my journal I have written that four of the women who came forward were miraculously healed as the tumors completely vanished when prayed for! That was a great crusade.

—Robyn Tan, London, England

I believe that the release of harvester angels or signs and wonders angels is accelerating at this hour. Many people who preach the true Gospel, the Gospel of the Kingdom, will actually have encounters with these mighty harvester angels. There are examples of massive angels in the Scriptures (see 2 Kings 19:15-16; 2 Sam. 24:17).

Normal Angelic Encounters

As you know by now, angelic encounters do not always have to be "super-spiritual" experiences. It *is* really wonderful when angelic encounters are life-changing. However, angelic encounters can be very ordinary at times. The Lord has a plethora of angels that are ready, willing, and able to minister to you in your everyday life. We can all expect to experience "normal angelic encounters." In reality, you are most likely experiencing angelic ministry in your life now, but are not aware of it.

We have an acquaintance who shared a humorous testimony about a "normal angelic encounter." Our neighbor had been traveling extensively and returned home after a very demanding trip. He was thankful to be in his bed, and as he lay down he thought, *Lord, I wish someone would massage my sore feet.* It was late at night, and he was ready to have a good night's sleep.

He was just about to fall asleep when he felt the comforter being pulled back from his feet. Half asleep, he felt a pair of hands take a strong grip on his feet and begin to rub them. He stirred and looked down at the foot of his bed where he saw a large angel massaging his feet. In a flash, fear gripped him as he jerked his knees up under his chin staring at the angel who was still standing at the foot of his bed. He yelled at the angel, "What are you doing?" The angel yelled back at him, "I am ministering to you!" then disappeared.

When Kathy and I were building our home in the mountains of Moravian Falls, I also experienced a similar angelic visitation. Kathy was in Washington state visiting our children, and I had purposed in my heart to stay behind to work on the new log home. I had invested several late nights, often working until 2 A.M. During those times alone in the mountains, the level of angelic activity escalated. It began to be fearful for me to be alone in the mountains at night as I worked on the house. But I decided that it would be better for me to just sleep at the house so that I could get an early start in the morning.

This particular night I worked until 2:30 A.M. Being totally exhausted, I went upstairs to the bedroom where I had placed my makeshift bed. In the darkness I could discern angelic activity, and streams of light began to shoot through the bedroom. A holy fear crept into my spirit, and I realized that there were a lot of angels close by. Still, I had purposed to sleep in the new house overnight. I decided to read my Bible by a flashlight. I finally fell into a deep sleep with my travel Bible open across my chest, asking the Lord if we had indeed made the right decision to move from Kansas City to the mountains of North Carolina.

At about 4 A.M., I was shocked into consciousness by the manifest glory of God and awoke to find the fear of the Lord hanging thickly in the room. There was a supernatural light illuminating the room, and every hair on my body seemed to be standing on end! Suddenly I saw an angel standing at the foot of my cot. This angel was emanating a glow and staring at me from under very bushy eyebrows. His gaze was fierce. It appeared that the angel was dressed in colonial clothing with a large hat and a big buckle on his wide belt. In his hands was what I can only describe as a book or ledger of some type. The angel glanced back and forth between the book and me several times. The pages of the book were flipping by very quickly like the wings of a hummingbird.

Suddenly the angel took his right index finger and quickly pressed it into the book, stopping the pages from turning. Then he looked at me, and then glanced back at the book where his finger was now resting. The angel looked back at me, and then he smiled at me and said, "You are welcome here!" I was totally conscious during this, and the words the angel spoke were audible to my natural ears. I had been staring at the angel, mesmerized by his sudden appearance, for about ten seconds.

After he spoke, the angel instantly vanished, but the fear of the Lord was still hanging thickly in the unfinished room. I was gripped with fear, unable to move for a long time. That was the last night that I spent in our new home until the day that we moved in on November 17, 2008. However, I was also given a great peace knowing that we were in the Lord's perfect will by coming to Moravian Falls. It was comforting to have an angel welcome us into our new home.

Although some angelic encounters can be fearful and even terrifying, many times you will look back on such encounters and chuckle to yourself. This will happen more and more as you experience numerous angelic encounters and visitations. At first you may be terrified when angels appear, but later you will look at your initial angelic visitations and realize that they were actually normal and even amusing.

These testimonies are funny ones, but they illustrate a simple point. God cares about the tiniest things in our lives, and He is willing and able to send angels to help us with any of our needs. We can expect to have angels involved in every aspect of our lives. Not all of our angelic encounters need to be super spiritual. Many times angelic encounters are quite normal. Expect to have normal angelic encounters in your life too.

Chapter 18

THE EAGLE HAS LANDED

In the spring of 2007, Kathy and I began to have a very unusual visitor to our home in Kansas City, Missouri. An eagle began to roost in our backyard and gather fish from the lake there. The first few times I saw the eagle I was surprised, but not overwhelmed. After the eagle visited the fourth time, the Holy Spirit alerted me to the fact that this was not normal. The Lord instructed me to pray about the eagle's visitation. I began to realize that this phenomenon was highly unusual and considered that the eagle might be a sign and wonder.

In prayer the next morning I told the Lord that if this eagle was being sent by Him that I wanted a sign. I reverted to an Old Testament principle and "threw out a fleece" before the Lord (see Judg. 6:37-40). I said, "Jesus, if this eagle is from You, then I want to feed the bird a fish. Then I will take this seriously." Later that morning, I left my prayer closet and decided to go fishing. I loaded my fishing gear into a wheelbarrow to take it to the small pontoon boat that was on the lake. I was about halfway to the water when the eagle swooped down from a nearby tree and flew within five feet of my face. There was no way to miss seeing him. At that moment, the power of the Holy Spirit fell upon me, and I began to weep.

The eagle landed in a large tree at the edge of our yard and watched me intently as I loaded my gear onto the boat. I shoved off to fish with the Holy Spirit as my guide. His presence was tangible and strong, very much like the morning in Botwood when we walked together in the cool of the day. The Holy Spirit guided me to a place on the lake where a stump was sticking out of the water and told me to, "Cast your line on the right side of the boat." This was amazing! I continued to monitor the eagle. It seemed to be peering at me intently, watching my every move.

"FEED THE BIRD A FISH"

On the second cast I caught a healthy largemouth bass. My mind was racing as I remembered what I had told the Lord just an hour before, "Jesus, if this eagle is from You, then I want to feed the bird a fish." I turned the little pontoon boat around and trolled over by the bank in my backyard. I grabbed the bass and heaved it into the yard. It began to flop and flip around on the dry green grass. Immediately, the eagle launched itself and flew in a sweeping arch to impale the gyrating bass with its powerful talons. I was astonished. The eagle then landed in a tree that was near the water's edge, and I watched as he made a meal of the squirming bass.

I had been telling one of our friends who had been associated with the prophetic movement in Kansas City that an eagle was visiting our backyard. He is an avid outdoorsman and told me that it was highly unlikely that an eagle would be within the city limits. So he told me to call him the next time the eagle came. As I sat on the pontoon boat watching the eagle eat the bass, I called my friend on my cell phone. He told me that he was on his way to check out the eagle. Our friend arrived in time to witness the eagle and to see it finish its meal and fly off. Then I docked the pontoon boat by the large oak tree in our backyard and rushed into the house at 11200 Kensington Avenue.

We discussed my prayer that morning and the eagle's visits. My friend told me that he believed that the Lord was seeking to tell me something. He asked what dates the eagle began to visit. It was April 19 and 20, 2007. He told me to read Acts 4:19-20. Those Scriptures say, *"...Whether it is right in the sight of God to listen to you more than to God, you judge. For we cannot but speak the things which we have seen and heard."* After that day, I was certain that the Lord was surely trying to tell me something important, and I purposed in my heart to fast and pray until I received the revelation.

I had been fasting for three days when Jesus visited me in a dream and told me to "google the golden eagle." This dream was powerful and very real. I woke up and looked at the clock—it was 4:20 A.M. (see Acts 4:20). I got up and googled the golden eagle—researched the bird on the Internet from my computer. I was fascinated to see photographs of the same kind of bird that had been visiting our backyard. It was then that I realized that our visitor was an adolescent golden eagle. I am not an ornithologist, but I am certain our visitor was an adolescent golden eagle. I pressed into prayer and fasting, meditating on Acts 4:19-20 for the next three weeks. I read those two Scriptures hundreds of times. Finally, the Lord highlighted a section: *"We cannot but speak the things which we have seen and heard,"* (Acts 4:20), and I had an epiphany.

Peter and John were speaking not only about the crucifixion and the miracles they had witnessed while they walked with Jesus; they were speaking about the transfiguration. Jesus had taken them up on the mountain to open their eyes to both see and hear into the realm of the spirit. The gift of discerning of spirits was activated in the apostles' lives on that day. They saw the glorified Christ, and they also heard the audible voice of the Father. I understood that Jesus was a seer. That is how He could always see and hear what His Father was doing in Heaven (see John 5:19). I also received the revelation that the Lord wants His people to be seers too. He wants us to speak about the things which we see and hear in the realms of the spirit. He is activating people to be seers.

As I continued to press in to the Lord about these events, the Lord instructed me to begin to study the history of the last outpouring of His Spirit. I knew that Jesus was referring to the Toronto Blessing—a revival that started in 1994 in Canada where hundreds of thousands of people attended, and many witnessed supernatural events and accepted salvation. However, the Lord also told me to study the history of the Kansas City Prophets. I told the Lord that I really did not know how to go about this, and He said, "I will send you help." Within six hours, I was given a great deal of historical literature, some published and some unpublished, about the events that unfolded in Kansas City in the 1980s and '90s.

WE MUST LEARN FROM OUR HISTORY

A friend who was the personal assistant to one of the leaders of the church which hosted the Kansas City Prophets gave me dozens of files, unpublished letters, and notes to study. He told me that he had been saving the material for over a decade, and for some reason he felt that I may be able to use the literature. I was astonished. I studied this literature and many other sources of information as the Lord led me for several more weeks.

Of particular interest were letters that were never published. The literature also contained letters that were published and sent to hundreds of churches condemning the Kansas City Prophets. I began to see that there was a strong correlation between the Toronto Blessing, the Kansas City Prophets, and John Wimber and the Vineyard movement. The outpouring in Toronto was sparked on January 20, 1994, when John Arnott invited Randy Clark to speak at a four-day conference. The power of the Holy Spirit fell unexpectedly during those meetings at the Airport Vineyard.

The leadership decided to extend the meetings, and the outpouring at Toronto continues to touch lives around the globe today. However, when the power of God began to manifest in unusual ways, it led to a fracture within the church at that time. I was intrigued as to why the Lord would have me study these things. Finally, I began to realize that there were threads that interconnected all of these events. What did the Lord want to teach me from the history of the recent revivals?

I continued to press the Lord about this, and He said, "Those who do not know their history are doomed to repeat it." So I realized that this was a very important issue on the Lord's heart. I found the history fascinating as I dug into it even more. Because I happened to know a few people who were of the inner circle in these recent historical events, I was privileged to ask them a lot of questions.

The more that I investigated this recent period of church history, the more I realized how significant it was. However, I could not understand why the Lord was continuing to supernaturally reveal all these historical facts to me. I grew concerned and asked the Lord almost daily what He wanted me to do with all of this knowledge. One morning in my prayer closet, I asked Him again for about the thousandth time. Suddenly the Lord responded to my question in a very clear and possibly audible voice: "History is about to repeat itself. Don't get caught up in the whirlwind." I grabbed my notes and wrote those words down.

I continued to fast and pray all the more and developed a heavy burden for the Church. I realized if history was about to repeat itself, we were on the verge of a great outpouring of God's Spirit, so I rejoiced. However, I also knew that the last outpouring created a rift in the Body of Christ, and had split the church. I was very concerned and perplexed by what I had heard. This burden continued to grow in my spirit. I decided to seek the wisdom of godly counsel. I contacted another friend who had been a key leader in the church in

Kansas City when the Toronto Revival broke out in January, 1994. He had walked through the crisis that arose concerning the Kansas City Prophets, and the revival in Toronto. He had worked to bring healing from the negative consequences related to the conflict that spread far and wide fracturing the Church. Since my friend had personally helped to deal with the fracture and split in the church, I believed that he was in a position to give me some good advice and guidance in this situation. I hoped that he could give me further direction and revelation concerning what I was hearing from the Lord based upon his experience and wisdom.

We met at Starbucks on Stateline Avenue, and I shared my heart with my friend, telling him that I believed that we were on the verge of a great outpouring. However, I also told him that I was very concerned as I believed that history was about to repeat itself. He listened to me very quietly. When I told him exactly what I had heard, "History is about to repeat itself. Don't get caught in the whirlwind," I could not help but notice that his face turned a little white, and his eyes opened a bit wider. He told me that preceding the controversy that broke out in Kansas City, the leadership had been given several warnings about what was about to happen. People had dreams, trances, and visions that all had a similar message: "Be careful; a whirlwind is coming."

Soon, I realized that the golden eagle was indeed a sign and wonder. The golden eagle represented the seer anointing and the release of the gift of discerning of spirits. The fact that the eagle had landed in Kansas City led to the revelation that the Lord was about to release the prophetic gift of the seer anointing into many cities in a fresh and pristine way. We shared this prophetic message in many nations in 2007, encouraging people to examine their hearts to prepare for these outpourings. As we traveled, Kathy and I discovered that eagles were returning to many cities in the United States and throughout the world.

We were given a newspaper article about a pair of golden eagles that had set up housekeeping in one of the largest cities in the Netherlands. Golden eagles were being restored to health and were beginning to show up in cities worldwide. We noticed many media articles about this phenomenon. The restoration of eagles is a sign in the natural of what the Lord is doing in the spirit realm. The seer anointing is also beginning to be released and restored en masse in many cities and nations throughout the earth as the Holy Spirit pours out the gift of discerning of spirits. I will share more details about how I received that revelation in the next chapter.

Chapter 19

THE SEASON OF THE GOLDEN EAGLES

In late May 2007, I continued seeking the Lord about these unfolding events. I was praying in my prayer closet one sunny morning asking the Lord for guidance and wisdom. For a brief moment, I saw Jesus in the spirit. He was motioning to me to come to Him. Jesus was waving at me in the same manner that He had done in 2001. I simply said, "Yes, Lord." Immediately, I was catapulted through time and space. When I "touched down," Jesus was there to welcome me. The Lord embraced me tenderly.

The Lord indicated that we should sit down on a large granite bench that was near the edge of an immense precipice. I noticed that we were on an extremely high and beautiful mountain range. These magnificent mountains were colossal, and their great snow-capped peaks stretched far into the beautiful azure sky above. The heavenly mountains were superior in height even to the Himalayan mountain range on earth. In fact, I somehow realized that the Himalayas would only be considered small foothills compared to these heavenly giants. These mountains were absolutely gorgeous and spectacular to behold. What a great blessing it was to be with Jesus in this magnificent setting (see 2 Cor. 4:18).

The Lord was flanked by a familiar group of four angels. There were great golden eagles circling lazily in the beautiful, clear sky far above our heads. The eagles were awesome to behold and seemed to glide effortlessly as their wings caressed the heavenly winds that gently flowed in this special place. I became engrossed, gazing upon the vista's beauty for a long time. I had actually forgotten where I was. Suddenly one of the golden eagles screeched, and I was jarred back to my senses. Then I remembered the Lord was sitting beside me. I turned to see that Jesus was smiling at me graciously. His creation is magnificent!

With a sweeping gesture of His left hand, Jesus indicated the vista and said, "It is truly beautiful, isn't it?" The Lord continued, "I have invited you here to show you something." Jesus then took His right hand and pointed to one of the great mountains across from our position. It must have been hundreds of miles away. He asked, "Do you see?" I strained my eyes, but all I could see was the massive peak so far away. I was a little embarrassed that I did not see what Jesus was seeking to reveal to me.

LOOK AGAIN

The Lord said, "Look again." This time as I looked at the mountain, it was as if my eyes were suddenly able to magnify the view. It seemed as if I was looking through a telescope, and I could see the mountain very clearly.

"I see, Lord."

Jesus said, "Look again."

When I did, my vision magnified to a much greater degree, and I could see the crags of the mountain very well.

"Look a little higher," He said.

I saw an enormous eagle's nest. At that precise moment, I saw one of the magnificent golden eagles gently land on the brim of the nest. I could see the eagle clearly, but from this distance I was not able to make out any details.

Jesus pointed again saying, "Look again."

Again my vision was magnified by 100 degrees. I was able to see the golden eagle in great detail. I could actually see the brilliance of the bird's bright yellow pupils. The golden eagle turned its head, and I saw it look at me. I could actually see the pupil of the heavenly creature focus as it set its gaze in our direction. Then the eagle shrieked and launched into the air, soaring higher into the heavens. I was stunned at the astonishing and unbelievable anointing I had to "see" at that delightful moment.

The eagle's nest was massive. I remembered what I had learned about golden eagles. Since golden eagles mate for life, they return to the same nest annually and continue to add to their homes. As a result, some golden eagle nests grow to be extremely large. This nest seemed to be enormous. In fact, the heavenly golden eagle's nest was about 100 feet or more in diameter. As I pondered this, I became lost in my thoughts until Jesus interrupted by reflections.

"Look again," He said.

It seemed as if my ability to see greatly multiplied once again, and I could now see the golden eagle's nest in great and minute detail. I saw eggs—not one or two or a few; there were hundreds and hundreds of golden eagle eggs. I was not only surprised but intrigued by this vision. Then I noticed that some of the eggs were beginning to wiggle and move slightly. As I continued to monitor the nest, I was surprised to see one of the golden eagle eggshells break as a small piece flaked off. Then I saw a small beak begin to emerge from the egg. Soon the egg rolled to its side, and I saw an eagle chick press its way free from the egg and hobble shakily onto the nest. At that moment, one of the golden eagles returned to nuzzle and inspect the eaglet gently with its beak.

Soon, I noticed that dozens of eggs were wiggling and moving. Within a few minutes, I saw several golden eagle chicks free themselves from the confines of the shells with an "egg tooth" and hobble weakly around the massive nest.

The Lord then said, "Listen."

I strained my ears and was able to hear the baby eaglets. They seemed to be chirping, but I could not hear them very clearly. Jesus told me to listen again, and my ability to hear was greatly multiplied. I could hear the golden eagle chicks cheeping, "Seers, seers, seers."

TRANSLATED THROUGH
TIME AND SPACE

Instantly, I journeyed in the spirit back to the night in Mwanza in 2001 when I had experienced the visitation of Jesus. I could feel my spirit accelerating through time and space. Suddenly I was reliving the vision that I experienced in the Tilapia Hotel. I was now in a vision within a vision. I was supernaturally hearing all the things that the Lord had told me that night about the seer anointing. Jesus had instructed me to study about the seer anointing in the Scriptures and to ponder that visitation in my heart until He told me to share it. My body was once more on the heavenly sand by the sea of glass-like crystal.

It was as if I was actually on the tile floor back in Africa. I was experiencing everything again. I saw hundreds of angels ascending and descending upon Jesus. The Lord was standing over me and speaking to me again about the seer anointing. After a long time the voice of the Lord launched me back through time and space. For a moment I was not sure where I was until I heard one of the great golden eagles shriek. In an instant I remembered that I was on the granite bench with Jesus by the immense precipice, and not on the celestial beach by the sea of glass-like crystal. The Lord was looking lovingly at me, and His beautiful smile brought me great comfort and peace.

The whole encounter and the supernatural ability that the Lord had imparted to me to see and hear so clearly were quite mind-blowing. I was stunned as I contemplated the things that I had just seen and heard. After quite some time, I knew that it was time to stand beside Jesus. We stood up together, and the Lord looked deeply into my eyes. For a moment, the power of His love was overwhelming, and I experienced it in the same way that I had felt it the first time that I had gone to Jesus in prayer. It was the same unconditional love I had experienced in Springdale, Canada, when He had stood over me on November 25, 2001. I was a little undone and was still having a difficult time comprehending everything that was transpiring (see Acts 4:19-20).

TIME TO SHARE

Jesus said, "The time has come for you to begin to share what I have shown you about My seers." Jesus then spoke many things into my heart. When Jesus finished His sayings, I was filled with revelation regarding the supernatural phenomena which I had just experienced. "Go now and write down the things that you have seen and heard. Remember that I am with you always, everywhere you go. Do not be afraid to share the things that I have shown you."

The Lord placed His hands upon my shoulders and looked deeply into my eyes again. He smiled at me and said, "Good bye for now." I found myself hurling through time and space again. I "reentered" my body in my prayer room in Kansas City to find myself covered with sweat. Tears were flowing from my eyes. I was not able to move for a long time. I stayed in the recliner in my prayer room and contemplated everything that I had just seen and experienced in my heart. After a while, I began to journal the events.

I have had a divine revelation that sovereign global outpourings of God's Spirit are headed to the earth. They will arrive much like the supernatural fireball surprised me in Canada. These global revivals will come in a most unexpected fashion and appear in the twinkle of an eye. There will be no way to stop what the Lord is about to do upon the earth. The Lord is about to release multiple outpourings of His Spirit.

There will be many revivals in many places. Cities will experience outpourings of God's mercy, love, and sovereign power. These cities or "pools of mercy" will be found on every continent on earth. The leaders of these revivals will not always be well-known; rather, many will be anonymous and humble. Many of the outpourings will be sparked by children and young people as they pray and seek the Lord with heart-felt repentance and fasting. Some of the greatest revivals will take place in individual hearts. Lone individuals will alter the future of regions and entire nations of the earth with their prayers as they experience a personal outpouring of God's love in their lives—and learn to work with God's angels.

Chapter 20

RESTORATION OF GIFTS AND THE APPROACHING GLOBAL REVIVALS

I t is important that we know our recent history because history is about to repeat itself. The Lord has been releasing a work of restoration within the Body of Christ (see Acts 3:21). We have seen the Lord restore most of the gifts of the Spirit over the last century or so. Let's look at a loose time line regarding restoration.

In 1906 with the Azusa Street revival, the gift of tongues and interpretation of tongues were restored.

In 1946, William Branham received an angelic visitation in response to his prayers. This angelic visitation sparked the Voice of Healing Movement which resulted in the gifts of miracles and healings being restored to the Church. This movement also activated the dormant gifts of the word of knowledge and word of wisdom.

In 1947, Gordon Lindsay sought to help Branham with his ministry. Recorded history confirms that William Branham operated extremely powerfully in the gift of prophecy, the word of wisdom, the word of knowledge, the gift of miracles, and healings. These gifts were activated as a direct result of well-documented angelic visitations.

Unfortunately, Branham fell into an incorrect doctrine later in his ministry; however, hundreds of other ministers were impacted by the restoration of these "power gifts" through the anointing that the Lord placed upon Branham. These ministers were activated or received impartations and began to operate in the gifts of the Spirit with great power and authority.

The Voice of Healing movement launched a healing revival in America and beyond from 1946 through the 1950s. Gordon Lindsay later helped to organize many of those men, including F.F. Bosworth, Kenneth E. Hagin, T.L. and Daisy Osborn, Jack Coe, Paul Cain, Ern Baxter, Jack Moore, A.A. Allen, Oral Roberts, and Billy Paul Branham to name a few. There were actually hundreds of men who ministered in the power of the Holy Spirit in association with the Voice of Healing Movement. Most of them ministered with the operation of all four of these "power gifts" evident in their lives.

In the 1950s, Kenneth E. Hagin received a visitation of Jesus Christ. The Lord commissioned Hagin to "teach My people about faith." Through the ministry of Kenneth E. Hagin and a few others, the gift of faith was restored to the Body of Christ during the 1950s and 1960s. Kenneth E. Hagin and Gordon Lindsay both finished their lives with grace and dignity.

I recommend Kenneth E. Hagin's book, *I Believe in Visions*. This book transformed my mindset when I first began to experience supernatural encounters with Jesus and His angels. It is a great resource, and not "hyper spiritual." Hagin's teachings in the book are very down-to-earth on the subject of supernatural encounters and visitations.

Beginning in 1948, the gift of prophecy was restored to the Body of Christ starting with the Latter Rain movement. Prophecy continued to develop in the Pentecostal movement, the Jesus Movement, and others through the late 1970s and into the '80s.

In 1982, the Vineyard movement was birthed through the ministry of John Wimber in California. The Vineyard brought the gift of prophecy into full bloom throughout much of the Body of Christ.

During this period, the gift of prophecy was beginning to be united again with the gift of healings. John Wimber was instrumental in taking the gifts of prophecy and the gift of healings to a new level in the Church. The Vineyard movement took these gifts of the Spirit to the nations. One of the aspects of the teachings of John Wimber was that anyone could be used by the Lord in the gifts of the Spirit.

From 1980 to roughly 1992, the Kansas City Prophets must also be credited for helping restore the gift of prophecy.

In 1994, John Arnott and his wife Carol were instrumental in stewarding the outpouring in Toronto, Canada, known as the Toronto Blessing. John and Carol Arnott are to be commended and honored for their humility and ability to follow the leading of the Holy Spirit. By allowing the Holy Spirit to have liberty in the midst of the outpouring,

Arnott modeled a sustainable model of how to steward the approaching global outpourings. The Toronto Blessing continues to impact the nations by training ordinary people to work with the gifts of prophecy and the working of miracles and healings. Many people and ministries have been powerfully touched by the Lord at Toronto Airport Christian Fellowship and have gone on to have an incredible impact in other nations and regions of the earth. There are many others; however, Roland and Heidi Baker of Iris Ministries in Mozambique have modeled how an anointing can be "caught" and taken to the ends of the earth. Thousands are being saved and touched through their ministry of love and power in East Africa.

Today the gift of discerning of spirits is being released and restored to the Church. We will see the release of this spiritual gift accelerate in coming days. The gift of discerning of spirits plays a very important role in the approaching global outpourings. Many ordinary people will become supernaturally empowered by this gift and begin to see and work with angels to impact the earth for God's glory.

SEERS

The Lord will birth and raise up seers throughout the earth. There will be thousands of seers who will come from every socioeconomic stratum. These seers will be empowered to see into the spirit and co-labor with God's angels. They will also operate in a spirit of wisdom and revelation. By unction of the Holy Spirit, they will know how to take advantage of the knowledge and revelation that they receive from the realms of Heaven. These will be ordinary people. Men, women, and children will be anointed to operate in the gift of discerning of spirits and the seer anointing.

Many of the seers are still developing, and many are immature or adolescent in their gifting. But the Lord has already begun to raise up people who are maturing in the seer anointing. They operate in the gift of discerning of spirits. Many are currently co-laboring with angels on a regular basis. Some of these forerunners will also operate in the office of teacher (see Eph. 4:11). They will train the young ones who are just beginning to walk in the seer anointing. The Lord will continue to raise up "Schools of the Spirit," or eagles' nests, throughout the earth.

These schools will train and equip seers, enabling them to grow and mature in the gift and ability to see. They will be given opportunities to massage and mature their spiritual gifts in safe and encouraging settings. These training centers will be established in every region. Pastor Bill Johnson has helped establish one such place at the Bethel School of Supernatural Ministry in Redding, California. That school is a great example of this kind of "equipping center."

One of the attributes of these seers is that they will have an incredible ability to see into the spiritual realm and then interact and work with the information they obtain. These people will also have an incredible ability to hear the Lord very clearly. This will be the outworking of Luke 11 and Matthew 6. These people will be able to see and hear what is transpiring in the heavenly realms and then have the privilege and authority to release it upon earth in the same manner that Jesus modeled for us.

This is a picture of the Cross. Seers will ascend vertically into the heavens and then release the revelation that they see and hear horizontally into the earth. Some people call this "third-heaven intercession." This type of revelation is also a type of the gift of the word of knowledge and the word of wisdom. It allows ordinary people to release on earth what is "relevant and real" in Heaven.

It Is a Time to Examine and Prepare Our Hearts

It is very important that we begin to examine our hearts at this hour. We are currently in a season of grace to check our foundations and the veiled agendas that may be hidden within the depths of our hearts. The Lord is currently shaking His people, preparing us for the approaching global outpourings. Everything that we have built that has not been founded upon the Rock of Jesus Christ will be shaken, and it will fall. We must all take the time to inspect our foundations and the hidden chambers of our hearts. The heart of the Church is not prepared to receive these outpourings yet. It is possible that some of these revivals may be fumbled unless we prepare and cleanse our hearts now. We must all be diligent to guard and examine our hearts in this area (see Ps. 51:10-14; 1 Sam. 16:7).

Two of the recurring stumbling blocks in all of the movements and revivals that we have looked at, with a few exceptions, are spiritual pride and idolatry. We must keep our singular focus on Jesus and Him alone. Our human nature is fallen. Our history is to exalt humankind within the Body and not the Head of the Body, Christ Jesus. This is true within the Church; we tend to exalt and worship man. This is idol worship. A scriptural example of this is found in First Samuel 8:5-6: "...*Now make us a king to judge us like all the nations. ...Give us a king to judge us....*"

God's people rejected Him as their King and chose a man. It is easy to see a man with our natural eyes, but it takes diligence to "see" and "hear" the Lord. This dynamic is still true of God's people today. It is inherent in our fallen human nature. We reject God and look to humanity. This leads to idol worship within the Church. This is why it is imperative that we seek to become transformed into the very image of Christ.

When we begin to exalt ministers and place them upon pedestals, that can become a form of idolatry. Instead of looking upon God, we begin to look at the men or women that God has anointed with power and gifts. This has been an element in the downfall of almost every revival and out-pouring in history. Individuals can become idols in our lives, minds, and hearts. We begin to put more faith in what the prophet, pastor, teacher, or evangelist says than in the holy Scriptures. Their words and ministries supplant our relationship with the Lord. It is possible for both ministers and the Body of Christ to be culpable in this matter, myself included. We should remember what the Bible tells us in Galatians 5:20-21: "...*Those who practice such things* [idolatry] *will not inherit the kingdom of God.*"

As a result of idolatry, we no longer pray to receive guidance from the Lord and become enslaved to the words of a man. It is easier to allow them to intercede and hear from

God on our behalf. We subconsciously begin to exalt and worship the man and not the Messiah. This is a foundational flaw in the "celebrity gospel" or "celebrity Christianity" that is prevalent throughout the earth today. We idolize personalities, and Jesus is no longer glorified. Many ministers are aware of this dynamic and guard their hearts against it. It is easy to slip into this satanic trap. Other ministers unwittingly embrace the glamour, glory, and idolization they receive from hurting people.

It is imperative that each of us develop an intimate and personal relationship with Jesus. It is dangerous to become dependent on others to guide our spiritual life no matter how anointed, visible, or popular they become. This was a key element in the downfall of the Voice of Healing movement and many other historical movements and revivals. The root of this "heart issue" can also be traced back to A.D. 313 when Constantine established the edict of Milan, which forever changed the face of Christianity and the dynamics within the Church.

During the first and second century, the Church was not fashioned in the manner that we see today. Most Christians met in homes or outdoors because there were not any church buildings. Believers in Christ met in informal settings, usually accompanied with a meal. Many times, they would meet around a low dinner table, and often as small groups that we might call "cell groups" today.

There was no "pastor" in these groups as we know today. Rather, the groups of believers relied on the Holy Spirit to direct the flow of meetings. Everyone was a pastor, so to speak, depending on the need of a given meeting. Individuals in a group would share or minister in their anointing or gift as the Holy Spirit led. Elders and apostles were available to help, but the fellowships were based on the concept of the "priesthood of all believers." It was a believers' ministry.

The Edict of Milan was responsible for the establishment of "edifices" or church buildings. Before that, believers met in homes. Church buildings, pulpits, and the concept of a priest (pastor) to lead religious meetings were incorporated and modeled after pagan temples, religions, and sects of the day. The pagan religions had high priests who led their meetings. Before A.D. 313, there were no church buildings or pastors as we know them today. This change opened the door to idol worship and witchcraft to infiltrate the Body of Christ.[1]

It is imperative that we keep our first love first and not allow our spirits to become lukewarm. God the Father, God the Son, and God the Holy Spirit must remain the absolute center of our faith. We must always move from a place of compassion and love of the Savior. When we begin to exalt the gift or the vessels who are carriers of the gifting, we may become guilty of idolatry. I would like to state this very clearly. *We need pastors.* I am not seeking to disparage the role of the pastor in today's churches. We need every ministry office outlined in Ephesians 4:11-12. Jesus gave us apostles, prophets, evangelists, pastors, and teachers. We desperately need them, but we need to understand that their role is to equip other folks for the work of ministry so that the Body can be built in fullness. Pastors were never meant to "do it all." It would benefit them to train others to help with the responsibility of overseeing the flock. We need pastors, but they were never designed to oversee or micromanage every aspect of the Church. The Church needs to be a living organism with a symbiotic, living relationship between all parts, working together to benefit everyone.

In the approaching global revivals, the Lord will begin to pour out His power and anointing through lay people. Some of the most powerful and anointed people on the planet will be totally unknown. God will not share His glory with a mere man or woman. When we begin to exalt others, we take Jesus off the throne and become guilty of idol worship. We must guard our hearts as God begins to pour out His power and anointing in the approaching global revivals. The Lord tells us that *"I am the Lord...and My glory I will not give to another, nor My praise to carved images* [idols]" (Isa. 42:8). The Lord could use a tin can or a stick to work miracles. In fact, He did (see Exod. 7:10; 15:25).

CHRIST: THE CORNERSTONE

I am not advocating any "new doctrine" or theology. Jesus Christ must be the absolute cornerstone and foundation of our faith in God. As such, we have the more sure word of prophecy, the standards that are laid out in the canon of Scripture that are to guide our faith. The Word of God clearly states that Jesus has given gifts to men (see Eph. 4:8). These gifts are released and orchestrated through the marvelous working of the precious Holy Spirit. The Lord will continue to anoint ordinary people with His Spirit and use them in the gifts of the Spirit with great effectiveness and success in the approaching global revivals. The anointing of the Holy Spirit is critical.

Scripture clearly establishes God's ongoing plan for the release of the gifts of the Spirit and His ministry offices. The imminent release of the gift of discerning of spirits and the resulting acceleration of angelic ministry will never supplant spiritual gifts or the anointing of the Holy Spirit. The restoration of the gift of discerning of spirits will complete the reestablishment of all nine spiritual gifts to the earth. (See Acts 3:21; First Corinthians 12:1,4-12; Ephesians 4:11-16.) As a result of the restoration of the gift of discerning of spirits, many will learn how to employ angels as they work humbly in symphony with the gifts of the Spirit, the anointing of the Holy Spirit, and the fivefold ministry.

We have seen from our testimonies how angelic ministry is closely connected with the gift of prophecy, the word of knowledge, the word of wisdom, the gifts of miracles, the gifts of healings, and especially the gift of discerning of spirits. Angelic ministry does not nor should it ever supersede the Holy Spirit's gifting. However, at times angelic ministry will work in harmony with the gifts of the Spirit. This will help empower us to minister in the Lord's spiritual gifts to release Christ's Kingdom upon the earth. Angelic ministry will be instrumental in ushering in the approaching global healing revivals. The Holy Spirit will work in symphony with angelic ministry. Angelic ministry will be just one more arrow in the quiver of your arsenal of supernatural weapons of warfare (see 2 Cor. 10:4).

This same kind of scenario will begin to repeat itself in many nations in the near future. God will employ angels to spark many of the approaching global outpourings of His Spirit. We will see an acceleration of God's people being divinely anointed with the gift of discerning of spirits. They will mature with understanding of how to interact and minister with the angelic realm that is already busily working around each of us. Prepare your heart! God's global revivals are on the way, and angelic ministry will be an essential part of these massive outpourings of the Lord's Spirit! God may also be preparing to use angels to spark a revival in your life too! Let's move to the conclusion of our journey together as we look at one more amazing testimony of an ordinary man who sees angels.

ENDNOTE

1. Frank Viola and George Barna, *Pagan Christianity?: Exploring the Roots of Our Church Practices* (Carol Stream, IL: Tyndale House Publishers, Inc., 2002), Chapter 2: "The Church Building; Inheriting An Edifice Complex"; Sid Roth, *The Incomplete Church: Unifying God's Children* (Shippensburg, PA: Destiny Image Publishers, Inc., 2007), Chapter 12 "Tradition."

Chapter 21

ACTIVATION AND IMPARTATION

There have been several aspects that many of our modern-day testimonies have had in common. The ability to see into the spirit was activated when the people came into a place where the heavens were opened or when they came into proximity with someone who was already operating in the gifting. This was also true of the servant of Elisha in Second Kings 6. This spiritual truth about seeing is illustrated beautifully in the life and ministry of Elisha. He prayed for his servant, and the man saw the angels that were surrounding them at that moment.

> *Elisha prayed, and said, "Lord, I pray, open his eyes that he may see." Then the Lord opened the eyes of the young man, and he saw. And behold, the mountain was full of horses and chariots of fire all around Elisha* (2 Kings 6:17).

Just as the angels were all around Elisha, there are times when the angels of the Lord are all around you too!

It's been said that "You cannot get the anointing from someone who does not have it." Elisha had it. Elisha had the ability to see into the realm of the spirit. He had the gift of discerning of spirits activated and in operation in his life. However, Elisha had much more than that. It is one thing to see angels; it is quite another to comprehend the methods and manner by which to employ the angels. Of course, Jesus had this authority, ability, and knowledge too. Elisha and Jesus lived under an open heaven.

When God opens your eyes to see into the spiritual realm, you are only experiencing elementary principles of the Kingdom. The Lord allows your eyes to be opened to see angels for a purpose. When we begin to understand this, then we are ready to begin to mature in the weightier matters of the Kingdom. We are then in a position to exercise our spiritual senses (see Heb. 5:14). We are then situated to begin to learn how to interact and work with angels to accomplish God's plans on earth and in our immediate sphere of influence.

It is important to massage your gifting to see and work with angels. You should seek opportunities to use the gifts and anointings you are given. Do not stop at the elementary things; don't settle for just seeing angels. The angels of the Lord are ready to work with you. Angels react with enthusiasm and become excited when you recognize them. But angels become ecstatic when you begin to employ them. Remember that Jesus has given you all authority in Heaven and earth. That means that you have the authority to work with and loose angels. Remember that Elisha received an impartation from Elijah; Elisha received a double portion! Elisha took his double portion to the river, and he smacked the water. You are going to need to smite the waters of your life too. You will need to activate the gift of discerning of spirits in your life and do something with it.

The ability to see angels is not something to take lightly. When you begin to see angels and operate in the gift of discerning of spirits, it is given to you for a purpose. Ultimately, that purpose is to exalt Jesus Christ. It is absolutely necessary that you learn to walk in nobility and humility just like Jesus. Remember that Jesus is your role model.

Let's prepare our hearts for the prayer of activation and impartation. Remember that *"...the testimony of Jesus is the spirit of prophecy"* (Rev. 19:10). Throughout this book, every testimony of angelic visitations and encounters are potential prophetic words for you to appropriate. As you have read this book, you have been preparing your heart and spirit to see.

We have seen people activated in the ability to see angels in many nations and cities as we have shared about angelic ministry. Sometimes seeing angels is as simple as believing and asking.

ABORIGINAL IMPARTATION

In 2004 I was in Melbourne ministering at a large conference called "Open Heavens Over Australia." The event was held on February 26th through 28th in the Melbourne Park Function Centre. I was part of the team that was praying for the sick during the altar ministry. On the first night during prayer time, a missionary woman brought several Aboriginals who were in need of miracles. One man was deaf in one ear. Another was Steve, and he was from the "outback."

I suddenly realized the healing angel had stepped up behind me. This greatly encouraged me as I was able to see that Steve was totally blind, so my heart leaped as I was sure that the Lord was going to heal Steve's blind eyes. I prayed for the deaf man first, and the Lord opened his deaf ear. Steve was standing close by, and I could sense that his faith was increasing. When I prayed for Steve, the anointing was very heavy, and I was sure that he was going to be healed. As I placed my hands upon his eyes, he screamed loudly, "I can see!" The scream caught me off guard, and I pulled my hands off of his eyes. He screamed again. "I can see the angel! I can see the angel; there is a big angel right behind you! I can really see that angel!"

Although blind from birth, Steve could also make out my outline as long as I stood close to him in the natural. However, in the spirit, he could see the healing angel. Every time I would lay my hands on his eyes, he would scream telling me more about the appearance of the angel that was behind me. This was amazing. I knew that the healing angel was standing behind me, but to have a totally blind man describe him was very special.

For the next 20 minutes I prayed for Steve several times. Finally, he just asked me to leave my hands on his eyes so he could "look at the angel." When I allowed my hands to rest on his eyes, he was able to describe the angel to me. When I would remove my hands and ask Steve to check his natural vision, it was growing a little better each time. But Steve was more interested in seeing the angel. Finally at the end of the first night, he was seeing in the spirit fairly clearly.

Steve and I became friends during those three days in Melbourne. We agreed to meet as many times as possible. I prayed for him many times. Almost every time I placed my hands on Steve's eyes, he screamed and shouted, "I can see the angel again!" His natural vision seemed to improve when we checked, but Steve was really happy that he could see the healing angel. It got to the point that when I would walk near him he would scream out, "Kevin's here; I can see God's angel!" By the end of the second day, Steve was beginning to see in the spirit more clearly. The gift of discerning of spirits was activating in his life. Remember, at times the ability to see God's angels can be a process.

This brings us to a very interesting point. Steve was totally blind in the natural. The healing of his natural eyes never did manifest. However, he was able to see into the spirit. Because of this experience, I can comfortably say that you can be blind and still see. Before I left Australia, I prayed about the incredible things that I experienced, as I prayed for Steve's eyes. I was 100 percent certain when I felt the healing angel step up behind me that the Lord was going to heal Steve. I was actually quite disappointed when He didn't. Honestly, after what I had experienced in Malawi, I was surprised that Steve was not healed. I was waiting on the Lord Saturday night and pondering these things in my heart. The Lord spoke to me very clearly, and I have never forgotten what the Holy Spirit told me.

The Lord said, "Steve is a prophetic picture of My Church."

I asked the Lord, "How can a blind aboriginal man possibly be a prophetic picture of Your Church?"

The Holy Spirit led me to Isaiah 6:9-10:

> *Go, and tell this people: 'Keep on hearing, but do not understand; keep on seeing, but do not perceive. Make the heart of this people dull, and their ears heavy, and shut their eyes; lest they see with their eyes, and hear with their ears, and understand with their heart, and return and be healed* (Isaiah 6:9-10).

Perhaps Steve is parabolic picture of the majority of God's people. We hear sounds in the natural realm, but we cannot hear or understand God's voice very well. We can see things with our natural eyes, but we cannot see or perceive with the eyes of our understanding. Most of us cannot see into the spiritual realm the way God desires for us. Perhaps our hearts are dull, and our ears are heavy. However, God earnestly desires for us to hear his voice and to see into His kingdom and to be healed. The Lord longs to empower you and me by His Spirit. We can see, touch, taste, and enter into Christ's Kingdom in this life. Sadly many of us do not. (See Luke 9:27; John 3:3; Psalm 34:8; John 3:5.)

From this experience, I have come to believe that the Lord prays for His people to see, hear, and perceive things from the spiritual realm, in addition to the things from the natural realm. I still remember the great big smile that would crease Steve's face when I touched his eyes. He shouted, "I can see the angels; I can see God's angels," and tears would flow down his cheeks. The last time I saw Steve, he told me it did not matter to him that he was still blind because "I see the angels. They are my friends." With that said, I watched as Steve turned and sauntered off with his walking stick in his hand and his feet slapping the floor.

That same night I was having another talk with God, "Lord, why didn't You heal Steve like You healed all of those other blind people in Africa and the blind intercessor in Las Vegas?" I had developed an emotional bond with the aboriginal man and really wanted to see him healed. I could not understand why his eyes did not open. The fact that he was not healed bewildered me. The angel was there, the anointing was there, and nearly every time the combinations of those two conditions had been present, the blind had been healed.

Finally the Lord said, "My son, Steve did receive his miracle. He *can* see." This statement brought tears to my eyes. I have often thought of Steve and his unusual miracle, and when I do, a great big smile grows across my face, and joy fills my heart. Somewhere in Australia, there is one blind aboriginal man who can see very clearly! Jesus tells us in Revelation 3:18:

> *I counsel you to buy from Me gold refined in the fire, that you may be rich; and white garments, that you may be clothed, that the shame of your nakedness may not be revealed; and anoint your eyes with eye salve, that you may see* (Revelation 3:18).

Steve's testimony substantiates that anyone can receive the gift of discerning of spirits and see angels. The impartation or activation is not just for the chosen vessels. Anyone can receive the gift to see into the realm of the spirit, even if they are blind. The angelic realm or dimension is available to all, whosoever will. If you have taken the time to read this book prayerfully, then you are also prepared and equipped to access an activation of your spirit. You are prepared to receive an impartation to see into the realm of the spirit and to see angels. You are in a position to have the gift of discerning of spirits activated in your life and "the eyes of your heart" open to see.

Take a few minutes to allow the Holy Spirit to minister to your heart before you pray. Ask the Lord to show you any areas that you may need to give to Him. If the Lord reveals any issues to you, then stop and wait upon Him as long as it takes to get the issue resolved through prayer and communion with the Holy Spirit.

Perhaps you do not know Jesus as your Savior. You can ask the Lord into your heart right now. Ask Jesus to forgive your sins and be the Lord of your life. (Read Romans 10:9-10; pray those Scriptures out loud over your life, and you will be born again—you will be saved, or born from above.)

Now wait silently. Then when you are ready, put into practice the number one key to activating the gift of discerning of spirits in your life. *Ask.*

PRAYER OF ACTIVATION

(Pray this aloud.)

Dear Father, I ask You now in the mighty name of Jesus Christ; Lord, I pray, open my eyes that I may see. Father, let Your Kingdom come. Let Your will be done here on earth and in my life as it is in Heaven. Lord, give to me the spirit of wisdom and revelation in the knowledge of Jesus.

Lord, I ask You to open my eyes to see. Lord Jesus, open the eyes of my heart today. Open my eyes, Lord, and allow me to see that those who are for me are more than those who are against me. Father, I ask You in the name of Jesus to open my eyes to see. Lord, let me see Your Kingdom. Lord, let me comprehend all that You have prepared for me. Oh God, open my eyes to see Your angels that are all around me. Lord, activate the spirit of wisdom and revelation in my spirit and in my heart.

Lord, let Your revelation come; let Your will be done. Lord, I am asking that You open the eyes of my heart to see the angelic realm that is all around me. Come, Holy Spirit. I ask You to guide me and teach me. Holy Spirit, I am asking You to manifest in the eyes of my heart. Lord, rip open the veil, remove the scales from my eyes, and let me see. Let me see into the spirit, and let me be free. Protect and keep me by covering me with the precious blood of Jesus Christ. Lord, open my eyes and anoint me to see. Amen.

Now take some time to wait on the Lord and allow the Holy Spirit to teach you. Let the Lord lead you, and embrace what the eyes of your understanding start to see!

Epilogue

The Lord is accelerating the release of angelic ministry on our planet. Many will be gifted to see the angels as the restoration of the gift of discerning of spirits comes into full fruition. The Lord has ordained this gift to be restored en masse at this hour. We have entered a *kairos* moment on the Lord's calendar. God's children will become aware of ways to work with Jesus' ever-present angelic hosts.

As we enter into this season, many of us will experience angelic encounters on a regular basis. It is important that we understand how to interact and co-labor with God's messengers. We will need to work in concert with angels and the divine revelation that they share with us as they visit the earth, or when we are allowed to visit them in the heavens. God's angels are our fellow servants of Christ Jesus, and we should welcome Jesus' angels.

The book that you are holding in your hands is a product of angelic intervention and ministry. On February 25, 2009, I experienced an angelic visitation at our ministry offices in Moravian Falls. It was eight years from the day I was born again. Jesus called me to Him in a time of prayer and assigned a third angel to me. The Lord told me this angel's name and that the angel was assigned to help me write. This scribe angel may be a resident of this geographical area. For the next 18 days I wrote almost ceaselessly with very little sleep, often writing overnight. Much of the material that you have read in this book was written during that time frame as the scribe angel stood behind and whispered into my left ear.

The approaching global healing revivals will surpass anything that society has experienced to date. Whole nations will turn to Jesus Christ overnight. Many of these revivals will be sparked by angelic ministry much like the Argentina Revival in 1949. In June of that year, a missionary, Edward Miller, working in the city of Mendoza, was led by the Lord to fast and pray for revival with a small group. Their prayers were answered with an angelic visitation that ignited an unprecedented outpouring of God's Spirit.

Two years later, in June 1951, a young man in City Bell, Argentina, was visited by an angel, and he started to earnestly repent for his sin. When that angel appeared, the power and conviction of the Holy Spirit fell, and the power of God swept through the region. The angel actually prophesied to that small group about the Lord's imminent plans to release revival into Argentina. These angelic visitations sparked a nationwide revival in Argentina. Later, in 1954, Tommy Hicks was invited to the nation to minister. Tommy Hicks was led by the Lord to approach President Juan Perón and ask permission to hold large healing crusades in the nation. Perón suffered from a serious skin condition and was healed as Tommy Hicks prayed for him.

This miracle resulted in Tommy Hicks receiving great favor from Perón's government, and he was given permission to conduct the crusade outreaches. He was given a stadium that held 60,000. Miracles and healings abounded in those extended meetings, and over one million people are reported to have attended. Tens of thousands were saved. This helped to transform Argentina.

These series of supernatural events were all sparked by those initial angelic visitations. I strongly recommend the book *Secrets of the Argentine Revival* by R. Edward Miller. This is a great resource for additional insight and understanding about how angels are impacting nations. This scenario will begin to repeat itself in many nations in the near future.

We are about to see the Lord release these kinds of "revival angels" throughout the earth (see Rev. 14:6). We will see the Lord release angelic agents of revival to every nation, tribe, tongue, and people. These angels will then co-labor with us to usher in the approaching global outpourings. This will mirror what happened in Argentina, as God will use ordinary people to spark national revivals.

These revivals will be notable because of the extraordinary numbers and types of miracles, healings, and signs and wonders that will be manifested for the world to witness via digital and electronic media. Another aspect of these global revivals will be the healing of incurable sickness and diseases like AIDS/HIV. Healing angels will be involved with these kinds of special miracles. Revival angels will work with many of us to release these types of miracles. The Lord will also anoint children to work special miracles.

The healing of AIDS will be especially pronounced on the African continent as God will raise up powerful evangelists from the children who will partner with the Holy Spirit and

God's angels to release mighty miracles and revivals to whole groups, tribes, and nations. Asia and China will be important areas where ordinary people will partner with angels to release God's power and usher in outpourings of God's Spirit. God will use many women and children to spark outpourings in China. Women and children will also be used in this manner in Afghanistan and throughout the Middle East to bring similar revivals.

Millions will be brought into the Kingdom through these imminent outpourings of God's Spirit. One of the current leaders of the Argentina Revival said that one of the reasons that the Argentineans see so many more salvations, miracles, and healings is because they embrace the ministry of angels. They believe that they can co-labor with the Lord's angelic hosts.

Many in the Western Church are unwilling to overcome their fear of the unknown and embrace the possibility of working with angels. These approaching global revivals will be ushered in by ordinary people who will overcome the fear of man and of the unknown to operate in the gift of discerning of spirits and the seer anointing. They will begin to embrace their inherent ability to work with angels. It is critical that we begin to open up our hearts and embrace angelic ministry at this hour because of its importance to the approaching global outpourings.

Stadiums throughout the earth will be filled because the power of God will be present to heal. At times there will not be any sessions—the revival meetings will continue without ceasing. The meetings will carry on nonstop, 24 hours a day, for weeks at a time. The miracles and salvations will flow ceaselessly because it will not matter who is on the platform releasing the miracles.

The Lord will continue to visit many Muslims in their dreams. Jesus will raise up many Christian evangelists within the Muslim nations as the result of "God dreams" that will be planted in people as a result of angelic visitations.

There will be thousands of unknown miracle workers who will partner with the Holy Spirit and at times God's angels to release God's miraculous touch in these meetings. The people will not care who is speaking because they will know that Jesus is in the house. Some of the most powerful and anointed people on the planet will be totally unknown. Jesus will be exalted and receive all the glory, honor, and praise. The people's eyes will no longer be on man, but on the God of man, Jesus Christ. Other revivals and outpourings will be smaller in scope and hidden from the eyes of the world. These local outpourings are very important to God's plans and will have an anonymous, but enormous impact on world events.

Many in the Body of Christ are being purged, cleansed, and prepared at this season. We must submit to the Lord's refining process to become God's friends. We must allow the Holy Spirit to renew our minds and have our hearts and thoughts transformed into the mind and image of Christ. As we allow the Lord to renew our mind and mind-set, we can begin to open the realms of Heaven over our lives. This in turn will give us free access into the domain where angels dance, worship, and minister. (We will examine how Jesus Himself has empowered you and I to open the heavens over our lives in the second book of this trilogy.)

As our minds become renewed, realigned, and set upon things above, we will see an acceleration of people being divinely anointed with the gift of discerning of spirits. They will grow and mature with understanding of how to minister with the angelic realm that is already busily working around each of us. Many of these lay people will begin to operate in the "power gifts" of the Holy Spirit to release miracles, healings, signs, and wonders. They will give all the glory to Christ Jesus. God is releasing a sovereign healing in the hearts of people, cleansing us and preparing us for His presence. He is calling many into this refining process today. I pray that you allow the Lord to prepare your heart to receive these massive outpourings of the Lord's presence and His unconditional love!

If you have enjoyed reading *Dancing With Angels 1: How to Work With the Angels in Your Life,* be sure to look for the next two books in this trilogy, *The Reality of Angelic Ministry Today,* coming soon from Destiny Image America. Our next adventure into the supernatural is *Dancing With Angels 2: The Role of the Holy Spirit and Open Heavens in Activating Your Angelic Visitations.* And later we will explore the realms of Heaven together in the third book of this fascinating trilogy: *Dancing With Angels 3: Angels in the Realms of Heaven.* You can order these books directly from King of Glory Ministries International's Web page, from Destiny Image America, or from many fine book retailers near you.

We are also working to compile our readers' testimonies of angelic encounters as they have activated angelic visitations in their lives after reading this series. If you have an angelic visitation or testimony that you would like for us to consider for future publication, please contact King of Glory Ministries International directly using the address listed in the back of this book.

Recommended Reading

I Believe in Visions
by Kenneth E. Hagin (Faith Library Publications)

Good Morning, Holy Spirit
by Benny Hinn (Thomas Nelson Publishers)

Secrets of the Argentine Revival
by R. Edward Miller (Peniel Publications)

Open My Eyes, Lord
by Gary Oates (Open Heaven Publications)

School of the Seers
by Jonathan Welton (Destiny Image Publishers)

Contact the Author

Kevin and Kathy would love to hear your testimonies about angelic encounters for possible use in future publications. To submit a testimony contact them by email.

King of Glory Ministries International is available to teach the material covered in this book in much greater depth in our School of the Supernatural—
Dancing With Angels
Understanding How You Can Work
With God's Angels.

This school is available on DVD and CD sets.

For more information, visit our Web page at
www.kingofgloryministries.org.

Email King of Glory Ministries International at
info@kingofgloryministries.org.

Call King of Glory Ministries International at
336-921-2825 or 816-225-8224

Or send us your mail at
King of Glory Ministries International
P.O. Box 903
Moravian Falls, NC 28654.

Please visit our online art gallery and help support our humanitarian outreaches by purchasing Kevin's artwork. In doing so, you help build orphanages for at-risk children and help us to feed widows and orphans in need. You may reach us at:

www.moravianfallsminiatureartgallery.com

A portion of all sales of art purchased from this site will be used to help feed orphans in third world nations. Thanks for your support in this worthwhile cause.

You can also donate directly to our orphanage projects in the third world. If you are a citizen of Canada, America, or the UK, you can give directly through Hope for the Nations, and your gift will be tax deductible in your home nation.

Look for the Hope for the Nations link on the King of Glory Ministries Web page, or surf to www.hope-forthenations.com.

Kevin and Kathy will be donating 90 percent of net proceeds from this book to those individuals and ministries who are building orphanages, helping widows and orphans, and preaching the Gospel to the poor and lost of the earth.

Your purchase of this book helps the cause. Thank you.

In the right hands, This Book will Change Lives!

Most of the people who need this message will not be looking for this book. To change their lives, you need to put a copy of this book in their hands.

> *But others (seeds) fell into good ground, and brought forth fruit, some a hundred-fold, some sixty-fold, some thirty-fold* (Matthew 13:8).

Our ministry is constantly seeking methods to find the good ground, the people who need this anointed message to change their lives. Will you help us reach these people?

> *Remember this—a farmer who plants only a few seeds will get a small crop. But the one who plants generously will get a generous crop* (2 Corinthians 9:6).

EXTEND THIS MINISTRY BY SOWING
3 BOOKS, 5 BOOKS, 10 BOOKS, **OR MORE TODAY,**
AND BECOME A LIFE CHANGER!

Thank you,

Don Nori Sr., Publisher
Destiny Image
Since 1982

DESTINY IMAGE PUBLISHERS, INC.

*"Speaking to the Purposes of God for This Generation
and for the Generations to Come."*

VISIT OUR NEW SITE HOME AT
WWW.DESTINYIMAGE.COM

FREE SUBSCRIPTION TO DI NEWSLETTER

Receive free unpublished articles by top DI authors, exclusive
discounts, and free downloads from our best and newest books.
Visit www.destinyimage.com to subscribe.

Write to: Destiny Image
                 P.O. Box 310
                 Shippensburg, PA 17257-0310

Call: 1-800-722-6774

Email: orders@destinyimage.com

For a complete list of our titles or to place an order
online, visit www.destinyimage.com.

FIND US ON FACEBOOK OR FOLLOW US ON TWITTER.

www.facebook.com/destinyimage   facebook
www.twitter.com/destinyimage   twitter